TRIBULATION
Closer Than We Think

An easy to understand
book on prophecy

Charlene Roberson Chandler

Roberson-Chandler Publishers
Moro, Arkansas

ACKNOWLEDGMENTS:

Permission is gratefully acknowledged from the following:

Scriptures designated NIV are quoted from the New International Version. Copyright 1973, 1978, 1984 International Bible Society. Used by permission of the Zondervan Corporation.
Scriptures designated KJV are quoted from the King James Bible.
All other Scriptures are quoted from The Living Bible.

References from The Works of Josephus, translated by William Whiston. Copyright 1987, Hendrickson Publishers, Inc. Used with permission.

References from The Zondervan Pictorial Bible Dictionary, by Merrill C. Tenney. Copyright 1963, 1964, 1967, Zondervan Publishing House. Used by permission of The Zondervan Corporation.

Quoted portions from The New English Bible, The Apocrypha, 1970, reprinted with the permission of Cambridge University Press.

References from There is a New World Coming, Copyright 1973. Hal Lindsey Ministries. Used by permission.

References from Foxe Book of Martyrs, by John Foxe, Copyright 1981. Used by permission of Whitaker House (www.whitakerhouse.com) Pages 18, 26, 28.

TRIBULATION
Closer Than We Think

An easy to understand book on prophecy

Copyright 2004 by Charlene Roberson Chandler
All rights reserved. This book, or parts thereof, may
not be reproduced in any form without permission.

Published 2004 by Roberson-Chandler Publishers,
Moro, Arkansas 72368
870-768-3479

Printed in the United States of America
Cover design and illustration by W.E. Hall

ISBN 0-9760895-0-5

Roberson-Chandler Publishers
Moro, Arkansas

To My Son
Mark

TABLE OF CONTENTS

1. How do We Know Christ is Lord	8
2. Lucifer, the Magnificent, Fallen	23
3. What is Sin	43
4. The Tragedy of Israel	46
5. Who are the Anti-Christ and False Prophet	66
6. The Great Tribulation	76
7. Between Death and Resurrection	105
8. The Resurrections	114
9. The Judgment Seat of Christ	119
10. The Second Coming of Christ	124
11. The Millennium	127
12. The Great White Throne Judgment	136
13. The Second Death and Hell	139
14. Eternity	150
Index	153
Endnotes	157

FORWARD

One beautiful sunshiny Saturday morning years ago in the 1960s, a delightful child of about seven or eight knocked on my door. Her name was Carrie Wiscerhofe and she wanted to tell me about God and how believing in Jesus could give us eternal life. She visited me several times after that and shared with me what she had learned about God.

We live in a world of religions. Religions, plural, because many say there are so many conflicting concepts and teachings that they do not know what to believe. This is the reason I humbly write for my son and set out in easy to follow chronology the minute knowledge I have acquired these many years studying as a teacher of Sunday school so he will not be misguided in what the Bible teaches about simple truths; that he, in turn, might teach his children that Christ is Lord and Saviour and understand the prophecies of the end time so that he, as well as all who read this book, hopefully will recognize that closer than we think is--The Great Tribulation!

CHAPTER 1
HOW DO WE KNOW THAT CHRIST IS LORD

A friend of mine once ended a speech with this: "It is difficult to convince some people there is a God. The rich say, 'If there is a God, I don't need him. I have everything.' And the poor say, 'If there is a God, where is he? Why does he not come to help us.'"

How can all mankind know there is a God and that Jesus Christ is Lord and Saviour? We who believe the Bible believe it was inspired by God, and the Bible says that Christ is Lord and Saviour of all and can give eternal life; therefore, it is so. But what about persons who say I do not believe the Bible? How can they know this truth? There are three ways, uncontroverted, undisputed, and without doubt that show us: By looking at the past, present, and future.

First, the past. We have history, not Biblical history but man's history; man's own compilation of human events that are accepted by all as fact that show that many ancient Bible prophecies have already been fulfilled.

Second, the present. Present world events show that many Old Testament as well as New Testament prophecies are being fulfilled today right before our own eyes.

And, third, the future. Current world events line up right on target to bring about the fulfillment of prophecies for the future of the end times and last days as the world relentlessly and inexorably moves toward the Second Coming of Christ and the Great Tribulation.

These days, we hear so much Biblical prophecy concerning the Second Coming of Christ but **what about the first coming of Christ?** Most of the Old Testament prophets were warning Israel of coming judgment and punishment because they worshiped heathen gods, but the prophet Isaiah who lived six to seven hundred years before Christ was born is known as the prophet of redemption and speaks of the Christ's first coming. Think about this, six or seven hundred years before it was to happen. History shows this prophecy was fulfilled with the birth of Christ (Luke 2:1-21). I might add at this point that it has been said that the test of a true prophet is whether or not his prophecies come true:

Therefore the Lord himself shall give you a sign. Behold, a virgin shall conceive, and bear a son, and shall call his name Immanuel. (Isaiah 7:14 KJV.)

Micah, one of the minor prophets of the 700s B.C. gives the prophecy as to the birthplace of Jesus. Of course, we all know from the history of Jesus that he was born in Bethlehem (Matthew 2:1-6), so Micah's prophecy was also fulfilled:

Bethlehem Ephratah, you are but a small Judean village, yet you will be the birthplace of my King who is alive from everlasting ages past! (Micah 5:2.)

Then there is this totally fascinating prophecy in which the prophet Daniel gives the number of years that were to pass before Christ's arrival upon the world scene the first time. The prophet Daniel was born about 621 B.C. During the reign of King Jehoiakim, King Nebuchadnezzar of Babylon attacked Jerusalem. Jehoiakim surrendered but Judah continued as a nation because Jehoiakim paid tribute to Nebuchadnezzar for three years (Daniel 1:1). It was during this first siege that Daniel was among the select hostages deported to Babylon in 605 B.C.[1] This is Daniel's prophecy. Listen to this!

(25) Now listen! It will be 49 years plus 434 years from the time the command is given to rebuild Jerusalem, until the Anointed One comes! Jerusalem's streets and walls will be rebuilt despite the perilous times. (26) After this period of 434 years, the Anointed One will be killed, his kingdom still unrealized .... (Daniel 9:25-26.)

Historically, after the destruction of Jerusalem and Solomon's temple by King Nebuchadnezzar of Babylon in 587 B.C., Babylon was conquered by Medo-Persia, and King Cyrus of Persia allowed some Jews to return to Jerusalem to begin rebuilding the Temple 49 years later in 538 B.C. (Ezra 1:1).

There is no Biblical history for almost 400 years before Christ was born between the ending of the Old Testament and the beginning of the New Testament. Therefore, it is not known exactly when the decree to rebuild Jerusalem was given, but 49 years plus 434 years equals 483 years, and Christ appeared right on time within the time frame of Daniel's prophecy.

Christ's trial and death is recorded in chapter 23 of Luke. History reveals he was also cut off, killed within this time frame, his kingdom yet unrealized. So this important prophecy has also been fulfilled.

With the birth of Christ, there arose a whole new religion called The Way (Acts 9:1-2) and also called a sect known as the Nazarenes (Acts 24:5). Totally contrary to Judaism teachings of adhering to the law, it taught that one might obtain eternal life through belief in Jesus Christ as Messiah and Lord and Saviour. It was at Antioch that believers were first called Christians (Acts 11:26).

We live in a "now world." If it doesn't happen today or tomorrow, many do not believe it will ever happen. Even hundreds of years ago, people did not comprehend fulfillment of prophecies pertinent to their day. The Jews knew the prophecies of the coming Messiah; yet, they refused to believe when it happened.

At the time of Christ's birth, the Jews looked for a political leader, someone who would restore Israel to power, prestige, and greatness. But the prophet Isaiah said it was not to be at Christ's first coming. Why? Because he came to die for the sins of mankind so that mankind might have eternal life. If Christ had not come and died for mankind, there would be no life after this one (John 3:16). It is that simple. Isaiah proclaims Christ's first coming as a suffering servant:

(1) See My Servant, whom I uphold, my Chosen One, in whom I delight. I have put my Spirit upon him; he will reveal justice to the nations of the world. (2) He will be gentle--he will not shout or quarrel in the streets. (Isaiah 42:1-2.)

(7) He was oppressed and he was afflicted, yet he never said a word. He was brought as a lamb to the slaughter; and as a sheep before her shearers is dumb, so he stood silent before the ones condemning him. (8) From prison and trial they led him away to his death. But who among the people of that day realized it was their sins that he was dying for--that he was suffering their punishment? (9) He was buried like a criminal in a rich man's grave; but he had done no wrong, and had never spoken an evil word. (Isaiah 53:7-9.)

The prophet Jeremiah[2] who is known as one of the greatest Hebrew prophets lived during the reign of King Josiah in 626 B.C. He gives the prophecy of Herod the Great killing the babies under two years of age after Christ was born because he feared him as a political king. Certainly King Herod knew the prophecies of the coming King of Kings. Herod the Great died in 4 B.C. shortly after the killing of the babies. The star guiding the Wise Men to Jesus was seen two years (Matthew 2:16) prior to that; so in all probability, Jesus was born about 6 B.C. This is Jeremiah's prophecy of this terrible act of Herod the Great.

The Lord spoke to me again saying, "In Ramah there is bitter weeping, Rachel is weeping for her children and she cannot be comforted, for they are gone." (Jeremiah 31:15.)

Ramah is believed to be an area just northwest of Jerusalem with Rachel in this context representing a symbolic mother. Remember that Jeremiah lived and gave the above prophecy approximately 600 years before Christ was born. New Testament writers were well acquainted with Old Testament prophecies. This prophecy was quoted by Matthew and was also fulfilled:

16) Herod was furious when he learned that the astrologers had disobeyed him. Sending soldiers to Bethlehem, he ordered them to kill every baby boy two years old and under, both in the town and on the nearby farms, for the astrologers had told him the star first appeared to them two years before.

(17) This brutal action of Herod's fulfilled the prophecy of Jeremiah, (18) "Screams of anguish come from Ramah, weeping unrestrained for her children, uncomforted--for they are dead." (Matthew 2:16-18.)

And God himself states that Christ is Lord and Saviour:

(6) The Lord, the King of Israel, says--yes, it is Israel's Redeemer, the Lord of Hosts, who says it--I am the First and Last; there is no other God. (Isaiah 44:6.)

And just as historians give eye-witness accounts of world events in history, Biblical historians who knew Christ give an eye-witness account of knowing him:

Christ was alive when the world began yet I myself have seen him with my own eyes and listened to him speak. I have touched him with my own hands. He is God's message of Life. (1 John 1:1.)

And the prophet Zechariah[3] of the 500s B.C. predicts Christ's triumphal entry into Jerusalem on a donkey's colt:

Rejoice greatly, O my people! Shout with joy! For look--your King is coming! He is the Righteous One, the Victor! Yet, he is lowly, riding on a donkey's colt. (Zechariah 9:9.)

This prophecy was also fulfilled. Matthew tells about this exciting event:

(1) As Jesus and the disciples approached Jerusalem and were near the town of Bethphage on the Mount of Olives, Jesus sent two of them into the village ahead. (2) Just as you enter, he said, "You will see a donkey tied there, with its colt beside it. Untie them and bring them here. (3) If anyone asks

you what you are doing, just say, 'The Master needs them, and there will be no trouble.'"

(4) This was done to fulfill the ancient prophecy, (5) "Tell Jerusalem her King is coming to her, riding humbly on a donkey's colt." (6) The two disciples did as Jesus said, (7) and brought the animal to him and threw their garments over the colt for him to ride on. (8) And some in the crowd threw down branches from the trees and spread them out before him.

(9) Then the crowds surged on ahead and pressed along behind shouting, "God bless King David's Son!"..... "God's Man is here!"..... "Bless him, Lord!"..... "Praise God in highest heaven."..... (10) The entire city of Jerusalem was stirred as he entered. "Who is this?" they asked. (11) And the crowds replied, "It's Jesus, the prophet from Nazareth up in Galilee." (Matthew 21:1-11.)

It is difficult for many to understand the chronology of Christ; that he was with God in all his glory before anything else existed or was created (John 17:5). He literally left his place of glory and became a mere human (Matthew 1:25) in this insignificant world, knowing he was to suffer and die for mankind (Matthew 26:24; Luke 23:26), believing and trusting God the Father to resurrect (Luke 24:6-7) and restore him to his former glory. Then after his resurrection, he ascended back to his place of glory where he is now at the right hand of God (Mark 16:19; Acts. 7:55; Colossians 3:1; Hebrews 10:12; 1 Peter 3:22).

Christ is also Creator of all things. It is explained in Colossians:

(15) Christ is the exact likeness of the unseen God. He existed before God made anything at all, and, in fact, (16) Christ himself is the Creator who made everything in heaven and earth, and the things we can see and the things we can't;

the spirit world with its kings and kingdoms, its rulers and authorities; all were made by Christ for his own use and glory. (Colossians 1:15-16.)

Many do not believe that spirit beings known as angels exist, but they not only exist but live in an organized order where each has his own status according to God's purposes. The spirit world as well as our world was created for Christ's own use and glory, and to serve God. **The purpose for our very being is also to serve God.**

This should answer the question of so many today that are searching for a meaning to life. When there seems to be no other meaning, serving God gives meaning to life. Why? Because of the life to come with God hereafter. Note that even the fallen angels, demons as we call them, not only knew Christ but acknowledged him here on earth. Of course they knew him. He created them. There is this interesting account of demons' acknowledgment of Christ:

(13) A team of itinerant Jews who were traveling from town to town casting out demons planned to experiment by using the name of the Lord Jesus. The incantation they decided on was this: "I adjure you by Jesus, whom Paul preaches, to come out!" (14) Seven sons of Sceva, a Jewish priest, were doing this. (15) But when they tried it on a man possessed by a demon, the demon replied, "I know Jesus, and I know Paul, but who are you?" And he leaped on two of them and beat them up, so that they fled out of his house naked and badly injured. (Acts 19:13-16.)

Luke also gives this account of demons' knowledge of Christ:

Once as he was teaching in the synagogue, a man possessed by a demon began shouting at Jesus, "Go away! We want nothing to do with you, Jesus from Nazareth. You have come to destroy us. I know who you are--the Holy Son of God." (Luke 4:33.)

Some were possessed by demons; and the demons came out at his command, shouting. "You are the Son of God." But because they knew he was the Christ, he stopped them and told them to be silent. (Luke 4:41.)

And a demon-possessed slave girl followed Paul and Silas around shouting:

..... *"These men are servants of God and they have come to tell you how to have your sins forgiven." (Acts 16:17.)*

Early Christian martyrs also attest to the fact that Christ is Lord and Saviour by their suffering through unspeakable cruelties. *Foxe's Book of Martyrs,*[4] by John Foxe, tells us that whatever cruelties man could devise, these were inflicted on the Christians: Whippings, scourging, stoning, burning hot plates of iron were laid on some, strangulation, the racks, drawings, tearings, and other barbaric tortures. Some were thrown to wild beasts as a spectacle in the amphitheatre.

Some were put into a hot iron chair and roasted, their bodies emitting a disgusting smell, while they died a prolonged and agonizing death. The Emperor Nero[5] used many for amusement by covering them with the skins of wild beasts and they were torn to pieces by dogs, while others were put on crosses, set on fire, and used as torches to light his gardens. But in spite of these continued persecutions, believers increased daily. No human being would endure such sufferings for just a mere man, but they endured and died for Christ, refusing to deny their Lord.

Crucifixion[6] was practiced by the Phoenicians, Carthaginians, Egyptians and then the Romans. It was one of the most cruel, brutal, and barbaric forms of death devised by man. In crucifixion, the victim was stripped, his arms spread and a heavy square spike driven through each wrist or hand into the crossbeam. The crossbeam was then hoisted and fastened to the upright pole already in the ground and a single spike was driven through the insteps of both feet, the slightest movement causing excruciating pain. The legs were cocked in such a manner that the victim was required to see-saw up and down on the spike in his feet just to be able to breathe.

Crucifixion is death by exhaustion and suffocation, slow and agonizing, the victim sometimes hanging for two or three days until he became too exhausted to push himself up and suffocated because he could no longer breathe. Sometimes the legs were broken so the victim could no longer push himself up to breathe in order to hasten death.

This is the brutal execution Christ suffered and died for mankind. It was a plan made even before the world or anything in it was created:

> *God chose him for this purpose long before the world began, but only recently was he brought into public view in these last days, as a blessing to you. (1 Peter 1:20.)*

> *It is he who saved us and chose us for his holy work; not because we deserved it but because that was his plan long before the world began--to show his love and kindness to us through Christ. (2 Timothy 1:9.)*

The Dispensation of the Age of Law ended with the birth of Christ, and the present age, the Age of Grace (Gospel Age; Church Age) began. This is explained in Romans:

> *For sin shall not have dominion over you, for you are not under the law, but under Grace. (Romans 6:14.)*

And Ephesians 2:5 (KJV) says this: *"..... by Grace ye are saved."* We who live in the Age of Grace are indeed blessed. Christ truly came the first time to give us eternal life. **Then if we can have eternal life through Christ, how do we gain it?** To gain eternal life, all anyone has to do is **believe** that Jesus Christ is the Son of God; that he gave up his place in glory and allowed himself to become a human being through being born a tiny baby to the virgin Mary (Matthew 1:23); that he did this in order to sacrifice himself through death on the cross for mankind's sins (John 3:16); that God the Father resurrected him and he came to life again on the third day after his death (Matthew 20:19); that he ascended back to his place of glory with God (Acts 1:9-11); that he will come again for us (Mark 13:26). This is confirmed through the following:

(25) Jesus said to her, "I am the resurrection and the life: he that believeth in me, though he were dead, yet shall he live." (John 11:25 KJV.)

But **believe in this context bears the connotation of constant commitment and strict adherence to the laws of God,** repenting of our sins and making Christ Lord of our life, rather than making just a single profession of belief in Christ. If we have made Christ Lord of our life, we have a genuine desire to live according to God's laws and follow Christ. This is what is meant by the much used phrase "giving one's life to Christ."

To **follow Christ** means to consciously and through a concerted effort turn from sin and living every day in a manner that glorifies him. This encompasses every aspect and area of our life: Living clean moral lives, being honest, never cheating anyone, forgiving others for injustices they have done us, how we act, how we talk--our speech which it has been said is the mirror of our soul, how we dress, whether we treat others with kindness whether they are husband, wife, family, friend or just people in all walks of life, fairness in all areas of our personal life as well as business transactions, even how we spend our leisure.

Many times in this day and age a watered-down version of Christianity is taught in which it is easy to be called a Christian, but true Christianity is not the easy life. It involves sacrificial living, giving up anything that is contrary to God's will and laws, even unto death:

Remain faithful even when facing death and I will give you the crown of life--an unending, glorious future. (Revelation 2:10.)

Does our daily life and actions reflect Christlike qualities? In self-evaluation, do we fit into the category of the true believer or follower of Christ? Any sacrifice made in the Christian life is so very small in comparison to the rewards. The true Christian and believer in Christ is awarded the gift unexcelled, the priceless gift of eternal life. This is explained in terms no one can misunderstand:

> *And God has reserved for his children the priceless gift of eternal life; it is kept in heaven for you, pure and undefiled, beyond the reach of change and decay. And God, in his mighty power, will make sure that you get there safely to receive it, because you are trusting him. It will be yours in that coming last day for all to see. So be truly glad! There is wonderful joy ahead, even though the going is rough for a while down here. (1 Peter 1:4-7.)*

And the Gospel of John states this:

> *I have written this to you who believe in the Son of God so that you may know you have eternal life. (1 John 5:13.)*

And Revelation has this message:

> *I, Jesus, have sent my angel to you to tell the churches all these things. I am both David's Root and his Descendant. I am the bright Morning Star. (Revelation 22:16.)*

If mankind could just grasp what eternal life really means, they would give up all they own to possess it. This is pointed out in the following parables:

> *(44) Again, the kingdom of heaven is like unto treasure hid in a field; the which when a man hath found, he hideth, and for joy thereof goeth and selleth all that he hath, and buyeth that field. (45) Again, the kingdom of heaven is like unto a merchant man seeking goodly pearls. (46) Who, when he*

had found one pearl of great price, went and sold all that he had, and bought it. (Matthew 13:44-46 KJV.)

The following quotation was copied from my Sunday school book in the early 1970s. Unfortunately, I do not remember who wrote it, but so impressed was I with its simple explanation of these parables that I have kept it all these years. This is what it said:

"The message of these two parables is simply that when man catches a glimpse of the kingdom life and realizes how it can become his, he is filled with a desire to have it at all costs."

And there is positive assurance that once eternal life is received, it can never be lost. No one can take it from us. It is ours forever and forever. Jesus himself emphasizes this:

(27) "My sheep hear my voice, and I know them, and they follow me." (28) And I give unto them eternal life; and they shall never perish, neither shall any man pluck them out of my hand. (29) My Father, which gave them to me, is greater than all; and no man is able to pluck them out of my Father's hand." (John 10:27-29 KJV.)

The danger is not in losing eternal life or salvation once it is received but the danger is in never having had it at all. Jesus emphatically states that there will be many who think they have gained eternal life but have not. He makes it abundantly clear that not everyone that profess to believe in him is a true believer, a true Christian. The life that reflects adherence to God's laws is outward proof of true Christianity. I cannot think of anything sadder than someone standing before Christ on judgment day thinking they are a true Christian and have him say, **"I never knew you."**

In the following parables, Jesus is talking to professing Christians, not lost humanity of the world. Notice that they call him Lord; yet, they do not know him:

"Not every one that saith unto me, 'Lord, Lord,' shall enter into the kingdom of heaven, but he that doeth the will of my Father which is in heaven. (22) Many will say to me in that day, 'Lord, Lord, have we not prophesied in thy name? and in thy name have cast out devils? and in thy name done many wonderful works?' (23) And then I will profess unto them, 'I never knew you: depart from me, ye that work iniquity.'" (Matthew 7:21-23 KJV.)

And then in the parable of the tares, Jesus further explains:

(19) "The hard path where some of the seeds fell represent the heart of a person who hears the Good News about the Kingdom and doesn't understand it; then Satan comes and snatches away the seeds from his heart.

(20) The shallow, rocky soil represents the heart of a man who hears the message and receives it with real joy, (21) but doesn't have much depth in his life, and the seeds don't root very deeply, and after a while when trouble comes, or persecution begins because of his beliefs, his enthusiasm fades, and he drops out.

(22) The ground covered with thistles represent a man who hears the message, but the cares of this life and his longing for money choke out God's Word, and he does less and less for God." (Matthew 13:19-22.)

Again, in the parable of the tares, Jesus explains how these superficial Christians (the tares) are to dwell among the true Christians (the wheat) until the harvest (judgment day):

"Let both grow together until the harvest: and in the time of harvest I will say to the reapers, gather ye together first the tares, and bind them in bundles to burn them: but gather the wheat into my barn." (Matthew 13:30 KJV.)

In the parable of the ten virgins, Jesus further emphasizes all professing Christians are not true believers or Christians:

(10) "And while they went to buy, the bridegroom came; and they that were ready went in with him to the marriage: and the door was shut. (11) Afterward came also the other virgins, saying, 'Lord, Lord, open to us.' (12) But he answered and said, 'Verily I say unto you, I know you not.'" (Matthew 25:10-12 KJV.)

Five filled their lamps with oil; five did not. All ten carried a lamp symbolizing a belief in Christ and were waiting for Christ to return, but only five had oil. The oil symbolizes the indwelling Holy Spirit in Christians. Half of them had no oil when the bridegroom came which indicates possibly as many as half who profess a belief in Christ are not true Christians.

Sin in the world is represented as darkness. True Christians are represented as light by the way they live and their impact upon the world. Without oil, a lamp has no light, and these five who had not filled their lamps were not true Christians. Their impact upon the world would be the same as a person walking through a dark room carrying a lamp with no light in it.

Only those who bear fruit are true Christians. Fruitfulness is a term used to define or describe how productive Christians are in service to God. False professors are non-productive and will be cut off, gathered up, and burned along with all other unbelievers at judgment day in the Second Death. Jesus specifically states "branch in me" that are to be cut off in referring to those who profess a superficial belief in him:

(2) "Every branch in me that beareth not fruit he taketh away.....(6) If a man abide not in me, he is cast forth as a branch, and is withered, and men gather them, and cast them into the fire, and they are burned." (John 15:2,6 KJV.)

The tragedy of today is that millions, the majority of world populace do not believe that Christ is Lord and Saviour of the world. Sadly, they do not even know the prophecies pertaining to his second coming; therefore, they do not recognize or see the fulfillment of prophecy when it happens. And when they hear the truth, they blind themselves by erroneous worldly teachings and refuse to see. According to prophecy, it is too late to save the world from judgment and punishment. The nations of the world today, just like Israel in the past, have failed to heed the prophecies of judgment and punishment. The have failed to heed the following admonition:

> *If my people, which are called by my name, shall humble themselves, and pray, and seek my face, and turn from their wicked ways, then will I hear from heaven, and will forgive their sin, and will heal their land. (2 Chronicles 7:14.)*

The nations of this world have not had their land healed nor have they turned wholly to God, putting things of this world before God. And just as Israel was judged and has been punished all through these hundreds of years including the Holocaust, so will the nations of this world today, including Israel, continue to be punished with war, disease, famine, crime, violence, earthquakes, volcanic eruptions, and floods which will worsen as time progresses, culminating in the holocausts during the prophesied Great Tribulation.

Old Testament prophecies were not written after Christ was born but hundreds of years before he appeared on the world scene. History confirms that Christ was born and died, a man so great that even time is dated before and after his life, and his followers have persevered all these hundreds of years. History and fulfillment of prophecy thus far has proven the authenticity of all these prophecies. This is how we know that Jesus Christ is Lord and Saviour.

CHAPTER 2

LUCIFER, THE MAGNIFICENT, FALLEN

*Mirror, mirror, on the wall,
who was the most beautiful
creature of them all?*

Lucifer! The name means the *shining one or bearer of light*. The Bible gives very little information about angels as individuals, but by looking in the 28th chapter of Ezekiel and the 14th chapter of Isaiah, a great deal can be learned about the beautiful creature Lucifer. Why learn about Lucifer? By studying about Lucifer, it is possible to learn about the origin of the Devil, Satan, and find the answer to the question that has been asked since time immemorial of why humanity suffers pain, sorrow, heartache, tragedy, and death in our world and why God allows such things to continue.

In Ezekiel chapter 28, Ezekiel is speaking of the King of Tyre but quickly switches to a description of Lucifer in verse 12. How do we know this? Certainly, the King of Tyre was never in Eden nor did he fit the description given of perfection and beauty herein. Here we are told of the great depths of Lucifer's splendor, grandeur, and power:

(12) ..... You were the perfection of wisdom and beauty. (13) You were in Eden, the garden of God; your clothing was bejeweled with every precious stone--ruby, topaz, diamond, chrysolite, onyx, jasper, sapphire, carbuncle, and emerald--all in beautiful settings of finest gold. They were given to you on the day you were created. (14) I appointed you to be the anointed guardian Cherub. You had access to the holy mountain of God. You walked among the stones of fire. (Ezekiel 28:12-14.)

Lucifer was the epitome of perfection. He was full of knowledge and wisdom, flawlessly perfect in beauty. He was covered in an array of the most gorgeous jewels. This beautiful covering was given him the day he was created. Lucifer was literally a rainbow of color--color reflecting the glory (light) of God as did no other created being. Think of the beautiful moon as it shines brilliantly just from the light that is reflected from the sun. Knowing how dull the moon's surface is, it is possible to just begin to comprehend what a tremendous light was reflected by Lucifer with his jeweled covering. It is no wonder that he was known as *the shining one, the bearer of light,* and *Son of the Morning* (Isaiah 14:12.)

Lucifer was also given special privileges. He had access to the holy mountain of God and walked among the stones of fire. Probably all angels do not have these privileges. The Bible does not explain what these are; but in *The Book of Enoch,*[7] Enoch describes such a place in his vision. Whether this is describing the holy mountain of God and stones of fire, we do not know:

> *(5) I saw the winds on the earth carrying the clouds: I saw the paths of the angels: I saw at the end of the earth the firmament of the heaven above. (6) And I proceeded and saw a place which burns day and night, where there are seven mountains of magnificent stones, three towards the east, and three towards the south. (7) And as for those towards the east, (one) was of colored stone, and one of pearl, and one of jacinth, and those towards the south of red stone. (8) But the middle one reached to heaven like the throne of God, of alabaster, and the summit of the throne was of sapphire. (XVIII 5-8 The Book of Enoch.)*

Who is Enoch? Enoch was the son of Jared and lived seven generations after Adam (Jude 14). Although the ancient writings of *The Book of Enoch*[8] are not included in the Bible, they are defined as apocalyptic literature by various authors but circulated under the name of Enoch. I Enoch was made through the Greek from original Hebrew text written by the Chasidim or Pharisees between 163-63 B.C. as the best source of Jewish doctrine for two pre-Christian centuries. II Enoch was written later in 1-50 A.D. Enoch was also identified in the Bible:

Enoch was sixty-five years old when his son Methuselah was born. Afterwards he lived another 300 years in fellowship with God and produced sons and daughters. Then when he was 365, and in constant touch with God, he disappeared, for God took him! (Genesis 5:21-24.)

Ezekiel also gives this description of a throne that was made of the beautiful sapphire stones:

(26) For high in the sky above them was what looked like a throne made of beautiful blue sapphire stones, and upon it sat someone who appeared to be a Man. (27,28) From his waist up, he seemed to be all glowing bronze, dazzling like fire; and from his waist down he seemed to be entirely flame, and there was a glowing halo like rainbow all around him. That was the way the glory of the Lord appeared to me. (Ezekiel 1:26-28.)

Lucifer was also in Eden. When we think of Eden, we think of Eden where God placed man when man was created. But *(13) Thou has been in Eden, the garden of God.....(14) Thou art the anointed Cherub that covereth, and I have set thee so.....(Ezekiel 28:13-14 KJV),* some Biblical scholars, specifically Alfred Thompson Eade in his *The Expanded Panorama Bible Study Course,*[9] interpret this to mean that this alludes to another Eden, an original Eden, a garden of God, which existed eons and eons of time in the past before man's creation and encompassed the whole earth, and God appointed Lucifer to be the anointed guardian Cherub over this whole creation.

Anointed means Divine Appointment and covereth means to guard. Mr. Eade's interpretation of an original Eden conjures up the fascinating picture that the earth in its original creation (Genesis 1:1) could have been created flawlessly perfect and inexpressibly beautiful, a perfect Eden, with no sun or moon, no days, years, or seasons, illuminated only by God's glory. How could it be possible to have light without a sun? Just as the New Earth will have no sun or moon during eternity because its light will come from the glory of God (Revelation 21:23-24).

Mr. Eade's interpretation, of course, necessitates separating Genesis 1:1 when the earth was first created from the seven-day Biblical account of the creations or restoration and refurbishing of an already existing earth starting in Genesis 1:3-5 with the first day consisting of just the illuminating of earth which is exactly what the Bible says:

(3) And God said, "Let there be light" and there was light. (5) And God called the light Day, and the darkness he called Night. And the evening and morning were the first day. (Genesis 1:3-5 KJV.)

Let me point out that it is an elementary deduction that this light in Genesis 1:3 that fell upon earth was not from our sun and did not pertain to one of our twenty-four hour days because our sun, moon, and stars were not made until the fourth day (Genesis 1:14-19) when God made and set them in place to be for signs, seasons, days, and years in our small galaxy.

Our galaxy is not small to man, but compared to other vast galaxies in the whole universe, our galaxy is minuscule. This means that three whole days of the creations (God's days) passed before our days began. Where then did this light in Genesis 1:3 come from that brought forth grass, fruit trees, and herbs (Genesis 1:11-13)? We can only speculate, but we know it came from God.

Under Mr. Eade's interpretation of another Eden in which Lucifer was anointed as the guardian Cherub prior to the Eden in which man was placed, it is the lack of Biblical knowledge concerning the vast expanse of time that apparently existed between Genesis 1:1 and Genesis 1:2 that creates the rift between scientific conclusion and most Biblical scholars' interpretation as to when the earth was created. Genesis 1:2 then describes the condition of the earth when God began the seven-day Biblical account of the creations, including man:

And the earth was without form and void, and darkness was upon the face of the deep. And the spirit of God moved upon the face of the waters. (Genesis 1:2 KJV.)

From a cursory reading of Genesis 1:2, it appears that this was the beginning of earth's creation and this describes one stage of the creation process which was immediately prior to the creation of man. But the Bible gives only basic elementary facts. It does not explain **how** God did the creating or **when**. Science can only theorize exactly when the beginning of the creation of the earth began, but most scientists believe the solar system and earth were created at the same time.

There are several theories about the formation of the earth,[10] but these are just theories. Eons are defined as long periods of time. Scientists claim the known history of earth's existence is composed of three eons, with four billion years composing the first two eons; that the earth existed billions of years prior to the appearance of man on the scene, with known civilization of man beginning only about ten thousand years ago. Scientists claim the dinosaurs lived in what is called the prehistoric Mesozoic Era some 220 billion years ago. These are elementary facts that anyone can get from almost any encyclopedia.

As far as man is concerned, there is tangible evidence of many civilizations of great wealth and power that have existed, some hundreds and some thousands of years ago, that have simply vanished and remain only in the faded pages of history. One of these was Sheba, now known as Yemen, which is located in the Southern part of the Arabian Peninsula by the Red Sea which was ruled by the Queen of Sheba in 900 B.C. She visited King Solomon and presented him with the largest gifts he had ever received, indicating great wealth (1 Kings 10:1-13).

According to Mr. Eade's interpretation, what Genesis 1:2 alludes to is, *"And the earth ....."* designating an already totally formed planet *"..... was without form and void ....."* The Hebrew words for *"without form and void"* are *tohu* and *bohu*[11] meaning desolation and emptiness. *Tohu* also means ruin. This describes the condition the earth was in immediately prior to the creation of man, and eons and eons of time and billions of years as scientists theorize could have passed between when God first created the whole vast

Universe, including the earth, and the time described in Genesis 1:2 of desolation, emptiness, ruin, and covered by water.

Alfred Thompson Eade bases his hypothesis on the following:

> *For thus saith the Lord that created the heavens; God himself that formed the earth and made it; he hath established it, he created it not in vain, he formed it to be inhabited: I am the Lord; and there is none else. (Isaiah 45:18 KJV.)*

The root word for vain is also *tohu*, meaning ruin, so the implication is that God did not create the earth in ruin as we see it in Genesis 1:2. Why then would earth be desolate, empty, flooded, and in a state of ruin? Under Mr. Eade's hypothesis, the answer is simple: Lucifer failed in his Divine Appointment as the anointed guardian Cherub. Because of pride, rebellion and disobedience to God, Lucifer brought judgment upon himself and his dominion. As the terrible wrath of the Living God fell upon the dominion of Lucifer, the earth became a desolate uninhabitable wasteland, dark and covered with water.

Since the earth was covered with water in Genesis 1:2, just as it was with The Flood in the days of Noah, it is also an elementary deduction that at least two terrible floods have befallen earth. It is no wonder that God was so emphatic in reassuring Noah that the earth would never again be made uninhabitable by water. Having been covered by water twice, God gave Noah and all future generations an everlasting covenant evidenced by the rainbow that he would never flood earth again (Genesis 9:8-17).

At this point, let me make it very clear to all who know me that Mr Eade's interpretation of Scripture that there was an original Eden which encompassed the whole world over which Lucifer presided before his Fall is not the doctrine of the church denomination to which I belong. But it is my personal opinion that it is the most realistic interpretation of the Scriptures that I have studied because it explains why Lucifer was in the Garden of Eden as the anointed guardian Cherub.

But most important, for the many who say I do not believe the Bible because science proves the Biblical account of the creations inaccurate, it reconciles scientific data that the earth could have existed for billions of years to the Biblical seven-day account of the creations concerning mankind as we know them in Genesis 1:3-31. Therefore, scientific knowledge does not disprove the Bible as much as it corroborates it. Man's scientific knowledge does not prove the Bible inaccurate but rather proves its accuracy under this hypothesis and interpretation of Scriptures by Alfred Thompson Eade that the earth could have existed as God's first Eden, as we measure time, unfathomable billions and billions of years ago in the dateless past.

The reason for Lucifer's failure and fall is described in Ezekiel:

(15) You were perfect in all you did from the day you were created until that time when wrong was found in you. (16) Your great wealth filled you with internal turmoil, and you sinned. Therefore, I cast you out of the mountain of God like a common sinner. I destroyed you, O overshadowing cherub, from the midst of the stones of fire. (17) Your heart was filled with pride because of all your beauty; you corrupted your wisdom for the sake of your splendor. (Ezekiel 28:15-17.)

Lucifer became so puffed up with pride that he believed that the beauty and light he radiated emanated from within himself rather than from God, and this pride led to his downfall. Isaiah explains how pride corrupted this beautiful creature:

(12) How are you fallen from heaven, O Lucifer, son of the morning! How are you cut down to the ground--mighty though you were against the nations of the world. (13) For you said to yourself, "I will ascend to heaven and rule the angels. I will take the highest throne. I will preside on the Mount of Assembly far away in the north. (14) I will climb to the highest heavens and be like the Most High." Isaiah 14:12-14.)

Lucifer fell because of pride. Lucifer wanted to rule the vast creation of all the angels when he said, *"I will ascend to heaven and rule the angels."* Lucifer wanted to be accountable to no one, not even God, when he said, *"I will take the highest throne."* Lucifer wanted to be like the Most High God. He coveted God's creations and wanted to make them his own.

For as he thinketh in his heart, so is he (Proverbs 23:7). No wonder our thoughts are so important. When we think good thoughts, it usually results in good; but if we hold wrong thoughts in our mind and dwell on them, it usually results in a wrongful act or works adversely against us. Lucifer's wrong thoughts led him toward a path of self-destruction. Lucifer turned from thoughts of God to thoughts of self; from God's glory to self-glory; from serving God to serving self.

There is no way of knowing how many eons and eons of time Lucifer existed in the spirit world prior to his anointing as guardian Cherub of Eden. But, *Thou was perfect in all thy ways from the day thou was created.....(Ezekiel 28:15 KJV.)* denotes that it must have been for quite some time. Surely, it was only after a great period of trial and testing in which he was found wanting in nothing that God anointed him, giving him his awesome power and the exalted position he held before his Fall. His power being so great that even the great archangel Michael did not dare criticize him:

> *Yet Michael, one of the mightiest of the angels, when he was arguing with Satan about Moses' body, did not dare to accuse even Satan, or jeer at him, but simply said, "The Lord rebuke you." (Jude 1:9.)*

Lucifer was only one of many in the vast creation of the angels. As stated in the previous chapter, Christ is Creator of all things, including the angels. He created them for his own use and glory:

> *(1) In the beginning was the Word, and the Word was with God, and the Word was God. (2)The same was in the*

beginning with God. (3) All things were made by him; and without him was not any thing made that was made. (John 1:1-3 KJV.)

And the **Word** was Jesus Christ. Simply explained, this states that God said, *"Let there be ....."* God the Father gave an order. Christ the Son carried out this order. He carried these orders to other heavenly beings; therefore, Christ became known as the Word of God. But when God gave the order for man to be made, he gave a different order: God said, *"Let us make man ....." (Genesis 1:26.)*

The creation of the great Host of Angels preceded earth's creation because angels sang and shouted for joy as earth was created (Job 38:4-7). The Bible is replete with the history of angels. It is also interesting that angels were created individually while mankind continues through procreation. Although they are spirit beings, they have form.

We are not told in whose likeness the angels were created, but varied descriptions are given throughout the Bible, and they did not all have the same physical appearance. Mostly, in the world today, angels are depicted as beautiful women, but angels mentioned in the Bible are always male. In the *Book of Enoch,*[12] Enoch gives the names of seven archangels:

(1) And these are the names of the holy angels who watch. (2) Uriel, one of the holy angels, who is over the world and over Tartarus. (3) Raphael, one of the holy angels, who is over the spirits of men. (4) Raguel, one of the holy angels who takes vengeance on the world of the luminaries. (5) Michael, one of the holy angels, to wit he that is set over the best part of mankind and over chaos. (6) Saraqael, one of the holy angels, who is set over the spirits who sin in the spirit. (7) Gabriel, one of the holy angels, who is over Paradise and the serpents and the Cherubim. (8) Remiel, one of the holy angels, whom God set over those who rise. (XX 1-8 The Book of Enoch.)

In many places in the Bible, angels are described only as angels of God; but in Exodus 3:2, an angel appeared in a flame of fire out of the midst of a bush. In Judges 13:6, Manoah's wife describes the countenance of the angel as very terrible. In Daniel 9:21 the angel Gabriel spoke to Daniel. And 2 Kings 19:35 states that a very powerful angel of the Lord killed 185,000 Assyrian troops.

In Joshua 5:13-15, it is no doubt Christ himself who appeared as Captain of the Host of angels because Joshua was told to remove his shoes because he was standing on holy ground. The angel Gabriel himself made many appearances delivering messages, one when he appeared to Mary in Luke 1:26-30. In Matthew 28:3, the angel's countenance was like lightning, and his clothing was white as snow. Revelation 14:6 depicts a flying angel. Luke 24:4 describes two angels as two men in shinning garments.

Isaiah 6:2 describes the Seraphim as an angel that has six wings; two wings to cover his face, two wings to cover his feet, and two wings with which to fly.

In Genesis 3:24 a Cherub with a flaming sword is guarding the Tree of Life in the Garden of Eden. Ezekiel 10:14 describes a Cherub as a being with large wings and four faces. The first face was of a Cherub, the second face was of a man, the third face was of a lion, and the fourth face was of an eagle. The Lord appeared in a vision to Ezekiel, a priest, the son of Buzi, who gives this amazing description of Cherubim attending the Lord:

(5) Then from the center of the cloud, four strange forms appeared that looked like men, (6) except that each had four faces and two pairs of wings! (7) Their legs were like those of men, but their feet were cloven like calves' feet, and shone like burnished brass. (8) And beneath each of their wings, I could see human hands.

(9) The four living beings were joined wing to wing, and they flew straight forward without turning. (10) Each had a face of a man (in front), with a lions's face on the right side (of his head), and the face of an ox on his left side, and the face

of an eagle at the back of his head! (11) Each had two pairs of wings spreading out from the middle of his back. One pair stretched out to attach to the wings of the living beings on each side, and the other pair covered his body.

(12) Wherever their spirit went they went, going straight forward without turning. (13) Going up and down among them were other forms that glowed like bright coals of fire or brilliant torches, and it was from these lightning flashed. (14) The living beings darted to and fro, swift as lightning.

(15) As I stared at all this, I saw four wheels on the ground beneath them, one wheel belonging to each. (16) The wheels looked as if they were made of polished amber and each wheel was constructed with a second wheel crosswise inside. (17) They could go in any of the four directions without having to face around.

(18) The four wheels had rims and spokes, and the rims were filled with eyes around their edges. (19,20,21) When the four living beings flew forward, the wheels moved forward with them. When they flew upward, the wheels went up too. When the living beings stopped the wheels stopped. For the spirit of the four living beings were in the wheels; so wherever their spirit went, the wheels and living beings went there too.

(22) The sky spreading out above them looked as though it were made of crystal; it was inexpressibly beautiful. (23) Each being's wings stretched straight out to touch the other's wings, and each had two wings covering his body. (24) And as they flew, their wings roared like waves against the shore, or like the voice of God, or like the shouting of a mighty army. When they stopped, they let down their wings. (Ezekiel 1:5-24.)

Daniel 7:10 and Revelation 5:11 reveals the great number of angels as being ten thousand times ten thousand and thousands and thousands. Millions of angels! Can anyone really comprehend the magnitude of such a creation as the spirit world. Think about it! God has millions of angels at his disposal to do His bidding. What a magnificent creation and organization that must be!

There are two distinct classifications of angels, holy and fallen angels. Holy angels are those who willingly do the perfect will of God. Fallen angels are described below:

And I remind you of those angels who were once pure and holy, but turned to a life of sin, now God has them chained up in prisons of darkness, waiting for the judgment day.(Jude 1:6.)

Many people, even many Christians have the magic-wand concept of God; that God just waved a wand and everything came into being. Scripture does not describe the creation of the spirit world, but for earth, plans and measurements were made and foundations were laid. How do we know? When Job complained to God, God asked him this:

Where were you when I laid the foundations of the earth? Tell me, if you know so much. Do you know how its dimensions were determined, and who did the surveying? What supports its foundations, and who laid its cornerstone, as the Morning Stars sang together and all the angels shouted for joy? (Job 38:4-7.)

Also in *The Book of Enoch*,[13] Enoch gives a fascinating description of his vision of his journey to see the mysteries of earth:

(1) I saw the treasuries of all the winds; I saw how He had furnished with them the whole creation and the firm foundations of the earth. (2) And I saw the cornerstone of the earth. I saw the four winds which bear [the earth and]

firmament of the heaven. (3) And I saw how the winds stretch out the vaults of heaven, and have their station between heaven and earth; these are the pillars of the heaven. (4) I saw the winds of heaven which turn and bring the circumference of the sun and all the stars to their setting. (5) I saw the winds on the earth carrying the clouds; I saw the paths of the angels; I saw at the end of the earth the firmament of the heaven above (XVIII 1-5 The Book of Enoch.)

Work was also involved in creating everything that was made. Genesis 2:2 states that God finished all the **work** he had been doing at the end of the sixth day. Most of us know the definition of the word work and we call a lot of things work; but for those of us who are old enough to remember the drudgery of spending a whole day just doing the family laundry by carrying buckets of water from the well, heating it in a heavy iron wash pot in the yard that you build a fire under, scrubbing clothes on what we now term an old-fashioned washboard, rinsing and wringing the water out by hand and then hanging them piece by piece on the clothes line to dry, know that there is a vast difference between actual working to accomplish something and waving a wand to accomplish the same thing; just as there is a vast difference between working by the old-fashioned method to do the laundry and turning the dial on the automatic washer and dryer, the wonderful equivalent of waving a magic wand.

As a child of nine or ten years old growing up during the Depression in Eastern Oklahoma between the beautiful Winding Stair and Kiamachi mountains, I remember being a happy little girl even though we were extremely poor, just like everyone else there. We had very few toys to play with, but there was always something interesting to do because there were mountains to climb, animals to play with, and creeks to play in.

Hills and trees and creeks with rocks and running water are wonderful things to a child. And then there were other assorted things children find to do in the country, especially for someone like me. Being very much a tomboy, I was playing cowboys and Indians and climbing trees with my three smaller brothers or cousins when

I wasn't playing house, dolls, jacks, coloring, or making mud pies with my sister Velma who was just older than I.

Now, making mud pies was one of my favorite pastimes; but even more than that, I liked making mud or clay animals. Clay was so much better than mud because it was so pliable; and when set in the sun, it would dry and stay for days without breaking. Sometimes we found clay in the wet creek banks with colorful red streaks running though it. My specialty in mud pastry was cinnamon rolls because the clay could be patted out very flat, sprinkled with white sand and then rolled and cut. I remember it as looking quite delicious even though it was inedible.

My favorite animal to make out of clay was a square horse with fat round legs, a head with tall ears attached with sticks through the clay, and a long tail hanging to the ground. To this day, I do not know my reasoning behind square horses other than a square body sits on legs much better than round bodies do.

And so as a child, I thought of God as making man in the same fashion as I made my horses; simply scooping up some dirt, molding a rough form of man, blowing on him and man instantaneously became a living human with all his coordinated component parts functioning perfectly, which God may have done just that. But Scripture only tells us **what** man is made of, just plain old dirt, not **how**. Of course, when I blew on my horses, nothing happened!

We are all aware that evolutionists say it didn't happen that way. It is entirely possibly that in dateless ages past ape-like creatures could have resembled man, even walking upright; but that does not confirm that they were human as evolutionists theorize. Nor is it important how God created man, except to point out that it only takes contact of one microscopic female egg and one male sperm to multiply into the billions of varied and complex cells, bones, teeth, eyes, et cetera that compose a perfectly formed baby. Therefore, the wonders of God are unfathomable in creating life and mankind.

In the *Life and Works of Flavius Josephus,*[14] Josephus, the renowned Jewish historian, in his translation of the creations from ancient writings of Moses, gives a little different and more detailed account of the creations than does the Bible, in that he says that before the Fall of Man all living creatures had one language and intimated that all communicated freely one with the other; that the serpent lived with Adam and Eve; but because he became envious of man living happily in obedience to the commands of God, the serpent with malicious intention sought to bring calamities upon man and persuaded Eve to taste of the Tree of Knowledge.

For man's disobedience, he was punished in that the ground would not bring forth its fruits of its own accord; woman was punished with the inconveniency of bleeding and sharp pains in bringing forth children, and the serpent was deprived of his speech and legs and had poison put under his tongue so he would forever be the enemy of man because of his malicious disposition toward Adam. And when God deprived the serpent of the use of his feet, he made him go rolling and dragging himself upon the ground; that because of the Fall of Man, animal life as well as man was changed forever. Man was removed to another place other than the Garden of Eden, and death became inevitable for all life forms. Josephus' account gives one interpretation of how the serpent was able to communicate with man (Genesis 3:1).

Most theologians agree that the Fall of Lucifer occurred before man was created. Theology presumes Satan to be the originator of sin in mankind; that Satan used the serpent to approach man; that Satan, in another deliberate act of rebellion against God, sought to destroy God's new creation, man. The question is then asked: Why would God deliberately refurbish the earth over which he had given Satan dominion (Luke 4:6) and place man in a position to be destroyed by the fallen, rebellious Lucifer who is now Satan? My conclusion is this: That from the very beginning God planned to test man, using Satan to test man's love, loyalty, and obedience to see who is worthy to live eternally with Him. This is pointed out by Peter:

> *These trials are only to test your faith, to see whether or not it is strong and pure. It is being tested as fire tests gold and purifies it--and your faith is far more precious to God than mere gold, so if your faith remains strong after being tried in*

the test tube of fiery trials, it will bring out much praise and glory and honor on the day of his return. (1 Peter 1:7.)

It appears that in the eternal plan of God that a certain amount of time was allotted for this purpose; therefore, this answers the question of why we have pain, suffering, sorrows, disease, and death; and why God allows these to continue for a time until his total plan is fulfilled. Just as childhood and youth are used to test and prepare us for adulthood, this short life span here on earth then is a test to see if we are worthy of eternal life with God. The testing of Job epitomizes the testing of mankind:

(6) One day as the angels came to present themselves before the Lord, Satan, the Accuser, came with them. (7) "Where have you come from?" the Lord asked Satan. And Satan replied, "From patrolling the earth." (8) Then the Lord asked Satan, "Have you noticed my servant Job? He is the finest man in all the earth--a good man who fears God and will have nothing to do with evil." (9) "Why shouldn't he, when you pay him so well?" Satan scoffed.(10) "You have always protected him and his home and his property from all harm. You have prospered everything he does--look how rich he is! No wonder he worships you! (11) But just take away his wealth, and you'll see him curse you to your face." (Job 1:6-11.)

Notice here that Satan is still accountable to God and has to give an account of himself and his activities concerning man, and his power is limited only to that which God gives him. Of course, we all know the story of the agonizing torments Satan inflicted on Job because God allowed Satan to test him. Satan was allowed to take away all his great riches and wealth, inflict agonizing pain upon his body, and even kill his ten children (Job 1:14-19; 2:7; 7:5) as a test of his faithfulness, but he remained faithful to God all through his physical pain, agony, and grief over his children.

Job gives a good example to follow because man cannot comprehend God's methods or the magnitude of what God has planned for him. The Bible is like a jigsaw puzzle as it was written by many different authors and in different time periods throughout history; but when the pieces are put together, a panorama of the ages unfold giving just a faint glimmer of the magnitude of God's creations and plans:

> *That is what is meant by the Scriptures which say that no mere man has ever seen, heard, or even imagined what wonderful things God has ready for those who love the Lord. (1 Corinthians 2:9.)*

If mankind could but grasp the glories God has prepared for him that he will receive after the trials of this life (Revelation 21:7), he would want to have this same relationship to God that the holy angels possess, putting the priority of living in perfect obedience to the will of God prior to the pursuits of worldly goals. Understand there is nothing wrong with worldly pursuits so long as they do not come before service to God. Because of the obedience of Christ who is the Prince of Peace (Isaiah 9:6), he is exalted. What a glorious future for Christ! His example should be followed!

> *(5) Your attitude should be the kind that was shown us by Jesus Christ, (6) who, though he was God did not demand and cling to his rights as God, (7) but laid aside his mighty power and glory, taking the disguise of a slave and becoming like men. (8) And he humbled himself even further, going so far as actually to die a criminal's death on a cross.*

> *(9) Yet it was because of this that God raised him up to the heights of heaven and gave him a name which is above every name, (10) that at the name of Jesus every knee shall bow in heaven and on earth and under the earth, (11) and every tongue shall confess that Jesus Christ is Lord, to the glory of God the Father. (Philippians 2:5-10.)*

Theoretically, if man had retained his state of innocence and perfectness in which he was created, he could have continued to live in a perpetual paradise without ever having to suffer any trials, testings, disease, pain, or even the heartbreak of death. This sounds very appealing! But through God's plan to test mankind after his Fall and then redeem him through Christ, God will exalt man's position to one he could never have attained in his original state. For believers will have the opportunity to not only judge the fallen angels but becoming co-rulers of the world during the Millennium (1 Corinthians 6:3).

A good example of this is to compare a baby or small child to an adult. If we remained a small child where we are loved, cared for, protected, and our every need met, we would go through our entire life being limited to the joys of a small child. But how many would want to remain in that state where they would miss all the greater joys of adulthood? Probably not many. Because by suffering through the growing, the trials, the heartache and the pain of life itself in becoming adults, we gain more than we lost. So it is with God's plan. God is giving man through trials and testings the opportunity to gain much more than he lost in Eden with the Fall of Man.

God made provision for mankind to be redeemed after he had fallen whereas Scripture does not state any provision was made for the redemption of fallen angels. Thus, the question has probably been asked many times: Why would the magnificent Lucifer deliberately choose a path of self-destruction knowing that he could not hope to win; knowing that in the end he would be defeated?

Yes, he knows that now, but did he know it when he first entertained thoughts of pride, rebellion, and of causing mankind's Fall? Probably not. God's plan of redemption and salvation was made even before the world or man was created (1 Peter 1:20; 2 Timothy 1:9), but it was a mystery that was hidden even from the angels:

(10) This salvation was something the prophets did not fully understand. Though they wrote about it, they had many questions as to what it all could mean. (11) They

wondered what the Spirit of Christ within them was talking about, for he told them to write down the events, since then, have happened to Christ: his suffering, and his great glory afterwards. And they wondered when and to whom all this would happen.

(12) They were finally told that these things would not occur during their lifetime, but long years later, during yours. And now at last this Good News has been plainly announced to all of us. It was preached to us in the power of the same heaven-sent Holy Spirit who spoke to them, and it is all so strange and wonderful that even the angels in heaven would give a great deal to know more about it. (1 Peter 1:10-12.)

Lucifer, now Satan, still has awesome power today. He is still known as the *prince of the world (John 12:31; 14:30; 16:11)* and *prince of the power of the air (Ephesians 2:2)* because he still has control over his followers. Think of what Lucifer's destiny could have been had he been obedient to God and retained his original perfection! This is the terrible punishment that befalls him, and all who know the prophecy are appalled at the fate of this beautiful creature!

..... Therefore I have cast you down to the ground and exposed you helpless before the curious gaze of kings. You defiled your holiness with lust for gain; therefore, I brought forth fire from your own actions and let it burn you to ashes upon the earth in the sight of all those watching you. All who know you are appalled at your fate; you are an example of horror; you are destroyed forever. (Ezekiel 28:17-19.)

Lucifer failed to fulfill the purpose for which he was created as the anointed guardian Cherub. He failed to retain the perfectness in which he was created. He who was the epitome of perfection became the epitome of evil; and instead of remaining the magnificent Lucifer living in total harmony with the will of God, he became

Satan, meaning adversary. He became God's adversary and enemy. Because of Lucifer's disobedience and rebellion against God, his destiny is judgment and the punishment of destruction forever in the Lake of Fire (Revelation 20:10). What a terrible fate for Lucifer! What a tragedy! Lucifer sinned!

CHAPTER 3
WHAT IS SIN

The word sin is derived from the Hebrew Word *hatta th*, a verb meaning *missing* and the Greek word *hamartia* meaning *missing the mark*.[15]

And man, just as Lucifer, through a willful act of disobedience, failed to retain the state of perfectness in which he was created. He lost the perfection of his original creation thereby missing the mark God set for him. What is God's mark? God's mark is perfection. Man is imperfect; therefore, man is a sinner regardless of how good he is as it is impossible to be perfect.

All mankind is missing the mark in some manner and come short of the glory of God (Romans 3:10; 3:23; 5:12); therefore, all are sinners. But what about the man who says, "I have lived a good life; I have done only good; I give to charities; I don't lie, cheat, steal, kill, or commit adultery. How can anyone say that I am a sinner?" The following explains:

> *And the person who keeps every law of God, but makes one little slip, is just as guilty as the person who has broken every law there is. (James 2:10.)*

It is because the results of sin are different and punishment is greater for some acts than for others that we tend to catagorize sin into either great or small sins. Thus it is said some are the greater sins because their results are so devastating. God is never against us; yet if we continue to sin, God lifts his hand of protection from us. One of God's ways of punishing here on earth is to let the natural result of sin take its course.

Sooner or later, sin produces its terrible result and that person's life is adversely touched or ruined by the consequences of his sin. Even worse, the tragic results of sin touches the lives of many, possibly affecting many generations. That is why the sins of the fathers are visited on children (subsequent generations) even unto the third and fourth generations (Exodus 20:5).

God may forgive even the most vicious murderer for his sinful act, but that does not alter the results or consequences of that sin. Forgiving the murderer does not restore the murdered person to life or remove his punishment for that crime, nor does it take away the grief suffered by those who not only love the person murdered, but those who love the murderer. God loves even the murderer because he is also one of his children. But how can anyone else love a murderer? Earthly parents still love their children even though they have committed murder.

In the early 1950s I lived in a West Texas town, Lubbock. A young girl Betty Fern White was strangled, and the papers were full of the pending execution by electrocution of a young man (I cannot remember his name) from nearby Reese Air Force Base who was the murderer.

As we at work read the Special Edition newspaper giving the gruesome details of the execution, including how the prisoner was prepared for execution by the shaving of his head and parts of his body, the paper included the account of his mother and brother flying back home just a few hours before the execution leaving the heartbreaking task of saying goodbye to her son to his lawyer. I was very young at the time; I think only about twenty-two and at that time had no son of my own, but I can still remember how my heart broke for that mother because she was so grief stricken she could not even say goodbye to her own son.

As a very little girl, perhaps five years old, I remember being taught in Sundays school about God loving all people the same, even the murderer. Now, I just could not understand how God could love a murderer as much as he did me because I was trying to be good. It was only when I had my own son that I began to understand. I do not love him just because he is good, nor would I stop loving him if he were bad. I simply love him; and nothing can diminish that love. But the difference for us in our children being good or bad is joy or heartache. When they are good, they bring great joy. But if they are bad, it brings indescribable grief and breaks our heart to see them suffering the consequences of their actions, their pain, heartache, and despair.

WHAT IS SIN

As a court reporter for sixteen years for the First Judicial Circuit in Arkansas, I sat in the courtroom and saw tears run down faces and heard the heartbreaking sobs of parents as their children, regardless of age, were sentenced for their crimes and led off to prison.

One of life's greatest tragedies is that the results of sin are not limited to the person who committed the sin. Also in the 1970s, a commentary in my Sunday school book had this shattering comment to make about sin. Unfortunately, I do not remember this author either, but its message has also remained with me all these years, and I have used it many times in teaching Sunday school. This is what it said:

> *"Sin has two results: (1) It separates man from God, and (2) it produces evil in the world. Forgiveness cancels the first, but the second must be borne by the sinner and those affected by his sin. Even when a man repents and is forgiven by God, the inevitable earthly consequences of sin relentlessly pursue the life of the sinner and those touched by his sin."*

One of life's greatest blessings is that God provided a remedy for the removal of sin through Christ. We shall not only have eternal life but will no more be subject to shame, guilt, or sin.

CHAPTER 4
THE TRAGEDY OF ISRAEL

Israel, God's chosen people, a special people called for the primary purpose of serving and worshiping God. Why then is Israel punished? We go back to the history of the rule of King David to find this answer.

Under the rule of King David (born 1040 B.C., died 970 B.C.),[16] Israel became a united kingdom consisting of the twelve original tribes originating from the twelve sons of Jacob. Jacob's name was changed to Israel (Genesis 35:10), so they are called the Nation Israel. God made the following covenant with David through the prophet Nathan:

> *(8) Now, go and give this message to David from the Lord of heaven: I chose you to be leader of my people Israel when you were a mere shepherd, tending your sheep in the pasture land. (9) I have been with you wherever you have gone and have destroyed your enemies. And I will make your name greater yet, so that you will be one of the most famous men in the world.*
>
> *10,11) I have selected a homeland for my people from which they will never have to move. It will be their own land where the heathen nations won't bother them as they did when the judges ruled my people.*
>
> *There will be no more wars against you, and your descendants shall rule this land for generations to come. (12) For when you die, I will put one of your sons upon your throne and I will make his kingdom strong. (13) He is the one who shall build me a temple. And I will continue his kingdom into eternity.*
>
> *(14) I will be his father and he shall be my son. If he sins, I will use other nations to punish him, (15) but my love and kindness shall not leave him as I took it from Saul, your*

predecessor. (16) Your family shall rule my kingdom forever. (2 Samuel 7:8-16.)

God made this same covenant or promise to David's son Solomon:

(4) And if thou wilt walk before me, as David thy father walked, in integrity of heart, and in uprightness, to do according to all that I have commanded thee, and will keep my statutes and my judgments, (5) then I will establish the throne of thy kingdom upon Israel forever as I promised to David thy father when I told him, 'One of your sons shall always be upon the throne of Israel.' (1 Kings 9:4-5 KJV.)

Walk in the above context literally means life-style; living according to God's will. Then there is the prophecy of what will happen to Israel if Solomon does not follow God:

(6) "However, if you or your children turn away from me and worship other gods and do not obey my laws, (7) then I will take away the people of Israel from this land which I have given them; I will take them from this temple which I have hallowed for my name and I will cast them out of my sight; and Israel will become a joke to the nations and an example and proverb of sudden disaster.

(8) This temple will become a heap of ruins, and everyone passing by will be amazed and will whistle with astonishment asking, "Why has the Lord done such things to this land and this temple?" (9) And the answer will be, "The people of Israel abandoned the Lord their God who brought them out of the land of Egypt; they worshiped other gods instead. That is why the Lord has brought this evil upon them." (1 Kings 9:6-9.)

From a study of the reign of King Solomon, Solomon did follow God during his younger years; but during his old age, he married foreign wives letting them bring in their foreign gods thus turning him away from God. This is the beginning of the destruction of the Nation Israel as God passes judgment on King Solomon:

> *(9) And the Lord was angry with Solomon because his heart was turned away from the Lord God of Israel which had appeared unto him twice. (10) And had commanded him concerning this thing that he should not go after other gods, but he kept not that which the Lord commanded.*
>
> *(11) Wherefore, the Lord said unto Solomon. "Forasmuch as this is done of thee, and thou has not kept my covenant and my statutes which I have commanded thee, I will surely rend the kingdom from thee and will give it to thy servant. (12) Notwithstanding in thy days I will not do it for David thy father's sake, but I will rend it out of the hand of thy son." (1 Kings 11:9-12 KJV.)*

When King Solomon died, the prophet Ahijah went to Jeroboam giving him this message:

> *(30) And Ahijah caught the new garment that was on him, and rent it in twelve pieces. (31) And he said to Jeroboam, take thee ten pieces: for thus saith the Lord, the God of Israel. Behold, I will rend the kingdom out of the hand of Solomon, and will give ten tribes to thee. (32) (But he shall have one tribe for my servant David's sake.....) (1 Kings 11:30-32 KJV.)*

Because of Solomon's sin of worshiping heathen gods, his descendants would not be allowed to rule the whole nation of Israel. The nation was divided into the Northern and Southern Kingdoms. Jeroboam was to rule the Northern Kingdom consisting of ten tribes, and Solomon's son Rehoboam was allowed to rule the Southern Kingdom consisting of two tribes, Judah and Benjamin. So the consequences of sin are reaching far into the next generations. But there was still hope at this point for Israel to continue forever as a nation even though it was divided. God made the same promise to Jeroboam that was made to David:

> *(38) If you will listen to what I tell you and walk in my path and do whatever I consider right, obeying my commandments as my servant David did, then I will bless you, and your descendants shall rule Israel forever. (I once made this same promise to David. (39) But because of Solomon's sin I will punish the descendants of David--though not forever.) (1 Kings 11:38-39.)*

But Jeroboam did not follow God. Instead he had two golden calves made. He erected one at Dan and one at Bethel (1 Kings 12:28-29). This, of course, was a great sin because the people worshiped them. And God pronounced this judgment on Jeroboam:

> *(10) I will bring disaster upon your home and will destroy all of your sons--this boy who is sick and all those who are well. I will sweep away your family as a stable hand shovels out manure. (11) I vow that those of your family who die in the city shall be eaten by dogs, and those who die in the field shall be eaten by birds. (1 Kings 14:10-11.)*

Because of his idolatry, Jeroboam's dynasty was cut off too, and his family members were not even given a proper burial. The judgment and punishment of the Northern Kingdom Israel for following King Jeroboam in idolatry was that they would be uprooted from the Promised Land God had given them and scattered across the world but that this scattering would not be permanent (1 Kings 14:14-16; Amos 9:8-10).

With each of the successive kings after Jeroboam, the kings continued to lead the people into idolatry, and the people followed the leadership of these kings until God could extend his mercy no longer and he swept them from his sight. The terrible destruction of the ten tribes of the Northern Kingdom is described below:

TRIBULATION, CLOSER THAN WE THINK

(5) Now the land of Israel was filled with Assyrian troops for three years besieging Samaria, the Capitol City of Israel. (6) Finally, in the ninth year of King Hoshea's reign, Samaria fell and the people of Israel were exiled to Assyria. They were placed in colonies in the city of Halah and along the banks of the Harbor River in Gozan and among the cities of the Medes.

(7) This disaster came upon the nation of Israel because the people worshiped other gods, thus sinning against the Lord their God who had brought them safely out of their slavery in Egypt. (8) They had followed the evil customs of the nations which the Lord had cast out before them. (9) The people of Israel had also secretly done many things that were wrong, and they had built altars to other gods throughout the land.

(10) They had placed obelisks and idols at the top of every hill and under every green tree, (11) and they had burned incense to the gods of the very nations which the Lord had cleared out of the land when Israel had come in. So the people of Israel had done many evil things, and the Lord was very angry. (12) Yes, they worshiped idols, despite the Lord's specific and repeated warnings.

(13) Again and again the Lord sent prophets to warn both Israel and Judah to turn from their evil ways. He had warned them to obey his commandments which he had given to their ancestors through these prophets, (14) but Israel wouldn't listen. The people were as stubborn as their ancestors and refused to believe in the Lord their God.

(15) They rejected his laws and covenant he had made with their ancestors, and despised all his warnings. In their foolishness, they worshiped heathen idols despite the Lord's stern warnings. (16) They defied all the commandments of the Lord their God and made two calves from molten gold.

THE TRAGEDY OF ISRAEL

They made detestable, shameful idols and worshiped Baal and the sun, moon, and stars.

(17) They even burned their own sons and daughters to death on the altars of Molech. They consulted fortune-tellers and used magic and sold themselves to evil. So the Lord was very angry. (18) He swept them from his sight and only the tribe of Judah remained in the land. (2 Kings 17:5-18.)

Conquered and defeated by the Assyrians in 722 B.C., Israel (the ten tribes of the Northern Kingdom) was destroyed, and only the tribe of Judah and Benjamin (the Southern Kingdom) remained. But judgment and punishment also fell on Judah. This is the reason:

(19) But even Judah refused to obey the commandments of the Lord their God. They too walked in the same evil paths as Israel had. (20) So the Lord rejected all the descendants of Jacob. He punished them by delivering them to their attackers until they were destroyed. (2 Kings 17:19-20.)

Judah was defeated in the final devastation of Jerusalem in 587 B.C. when King Nebuchadnezzar of Babylon attacked. And the Southern Kingdom was also destroyed (2 Kings 24:10). The tragic plunder that took place is also described:

(13) The Babylonians carried home all the treasures from the temple and the royal palace; and they cut apart all the gold bowls which King Solomon of Israel had placed in the Temple at the Lord's direction. (14) King Nebuchadnezzar took ten thousand captives from Jerusalem including all the princes and the best of the soldiers, craftsmen, and smiths, so only the poorest and least skilled people were left in the land. (15) Nebuchadnezzar took King Jehoiachin, his wives and officials, and the queen mother, to Babylon.....

(20) So the Lord finally in his anger, destroyed the people of Jerusalem and Judah. (2 Kings 24:13-15, 20.)

And all Israel ceased to exist as a nation.

Over and over again Israel turned away from God and was taken into captivity by other nations as punishment, and God delivered them out of bondage again and again. But if Israel had heeded the prophets and the prophecies, they would have known that this time was different; that the time had come when God would extend his mercy no longer, and (1) Israel would be punished again, (2) this punishment would be the longest, and (3) would be the most severe of all they had experienced thus far.

(1) What was this punishment? Total destruction of their holy city Jerusalem, their Temple, their nation, and being scattered across the world. But even in the midst of this punishment, Hosea 11:9 gives hope to Israel:

No, I will not punish you as much as my fierce anger tells me to. This is the last time I will destroy Ephraim .....(Hosea 11:9.) Meaning Israel.

(2) The longest punishment of Israel: This punishment has lasted hundreds and hundreds of years and will continue until Christ comes again and the Age of Grace has ended.

(3) The most severe punishment thus far of Israel: Continued persecution. This is the judgment God pronounced upon them:

(11) For I promise you: Because you have defiled my Temple with idols and evil sacrifices, therefore I will not spare you nor pity you at all. (12) One-third of you will die from famine and disease; one-third will be slaughtered by the enemy; and one-third I will scatter to the winds; sending the sword of the enemy chasing after you. (Ezekiel 5:11-12.)

THE TRAGEDY OF ISRAEL

Again Israel was enslaved and brought into captivity as they had been in Egypt. But in 539 B.C., the great Babylonian Empire crumbled when it was captured by the Medes and Persians (Isaiah 13:14-20). And during the first year of the reign of King Cyrus of Persia, 42,360 Jews were allowed to return to Jerusalem and rebuild the temple (Ezra 1:1-11, 2:1-64) under the direction of Zerubbabel; therefore, this second temple is referred to as Zerubbabel's temple.

The restoration of Israel again was begun, but Persia was conquered by Greece, and Greece was conquered by Rome. Israel was now under the Roman rule, and because the Jews rejected their Messiah, Christ, their punishment continued. Roman history reveals riots, widespread rebellion, and revolts of the Jews because of unsatisfactory procurators governing them under the rule of the Romans. These revolts were crushed by the Romans.

It was Gessius Florus[17] who was the procurator in A.D. 70; and through an abuse of his power, instigated the revolt that brought about the fall of Jerusalem and destruction of this second Jewish temple originally called Zerubbabel's temple. But Zerubbabel's temple, by this time, had become known as Herod's temple because Herod the Great, who was well known for his many building projects, enlarged and enhanced its appearance to magnificence and grandeur.

Flavius Vespanianus Titus[18] was born A.D. 39 and later succeeded his father in becoming emperor of Rome. He inherited and concluded the Jewish Wars in that final and devastating assault in A.D. 70.

Josephus, the renowned Jewish historian[19] gives a horrifying description of this siege: Jerusalem was fortified with three walls and built on two hills with a valley in between them; and in this valley, there was a spring of sweet water. The hills were surrounded by deep precipices on both sides making them impassable. The walls were ten cubits wide and twenty cubits high with towers and battlements. Above the towers were magnificent rooms with cisterns to catch rainwater.

An eye-witness account by Josephus is given of the conditions inside the city during the siege: Famine was everywhere. Priceless possessions were sold for a measure of wheat for the richer and barley for the poorer. So great was starvation that children snatched food from their father's mouths; and even worse, mothers took food from their infants.

The seditious and robbers in the city took all food from those who had risked their life going into the valley in search of food. Old men were beaten if they held onto their food, and the hair of women was torn out. They were barbarously cruel to those who ate the food before they could steal it and invented unspeakable methods of torments to discover where food was hidden such as stopping up their privy parts and driving stakes up their fundament.

Josephus says that never before had any city been subjected to such suffering and misery; the seditious and robbers were within the city and the Romans without. Titus ordered his troops to ambush all those who went into the valleys to gather food. The severity of famine created absolute necessity in going out, and five hundred Jews a day were captured.

Those caught were whipped and tormented with all sorts of torture and then crucified. The wrath and hatred of the soldiers was so great that they nailed some to the cross one way and others another way. There were so many crosses that there was no room for more. Titus pitied them but did not forbid it because he hoped this would cause those inside the city to surrender; but the seditious would not give in, nor would they let others escape.

Titus surrounded the city walls; and all hope of escape for the Jews was cut off, even into the valleys for food. Famine devoured whole houses and families; adults and children alike wandered around swollen with famine, falling dead wherever they were.

The seditious ordered the bodies to be buried because of the unbearable stench; but because there were too many, they had them thrown over the walls into the valley below. Titus groaned when he saw the valley full of dead bodies with thick putrefaction running about them; and wishing to spare those remaining of their miseries, he began preparing for another onslaught.

Deserters wishing to escape the famine and miseries of the seditious and robbers in the city leaped down from the wall; while some carrying stones pretended to fight, but fled to the Romans as

THE TRAGEDY OF ISRAEL

soon as they were outside the city. But an even worse fate awaited many of them. Many overfilled their swollen bodies with corn and burst.

As other deserters filled the many camps, a multitude of Arabians and Syrians cut into their bowels and searched their bellies for gold coins, as many Jews swallowed coins because the seditious searched everyone before they left the city. As many as two thousand Jews were dissected in a night in this barbarous treatment. And even though Titus, when he heard of this wicked practice, forbid it upon penalty of death, it continued in secret.

Josephus[20] continues with an eye-witness account of slaughter, bloodshed, and suffering, as the miseries in Jerusalem grew worse and worse as the Jews, in their desperate extremity, fought against insurmountable odds to defend their city and their temple, to bitter defeat. Eleven hundred thousand Jews died during this siege. Thousands upon thousands of these Jews starved, many being those who had come to Jerusalem from all parts of the country for the Feast of Unleavened Bread and suddenly found themselves shut in and imprisoned by the Roman army.

Josephus also relates the tragic disposition of the Jews who survived. Ninety-seven thousand Jews were captured. The seditious and robbers were killed; young and handsome men over age seventeen were reserved for the triumph; other men over age seventeen were sent into Egyptian mines; many were sent to other provinces to be killed in the theaters and sports arenas by sword or wild animals; and those under seventeen years of age were sold as slaves.

The Jews,[21] led by the false Messiah Bar Cochba revolted again against the Romans in A.D. 134, and what was left of Jerusalem was totally destroyed with even the foundations being plowed up. The Romans began rebuilding the city two years later, but excluded all Jews for two centuries until the reign of Constantine who was the first Roman emperor to become a Christian and allowed some Jews to return to Jerusalem.

For 2000 years, history has revealed the plight of the remaining one-third of the Jews who were scattered all over the world as prophecy after prophecy in Ezekiel 5:11, 7:25, the minor prophets, and 1 Kings 9:7-10 has been carried out as God literally lifted his hand of mercy and nation after nation sat by and watched continued persecution with the sword of the enemy indeed chasing after them with such atrocities as the Holocaust. Six million Jews were exterminated under the Hitler Regime.

Israel, with no land and no power, became a joke to the nations and an example and a proverb of sudden disaster as prophesied in 1 Kings 9:7. Their magnificent temple with all its treasures was plundered and destroyed becoming a heap of ruins. And many people, not knowing the history and prophecy of Israel, indeed ask, "If the Jew is God's chosen ones, why has he allowed such things to happen to them?"

The Apocrypha,[22] is defined as books of ancient writings of dubious authenticity not included in the Jewish or Protestant versions of the Old Testament but included in the Septuagint and editions of the Roman Catholic Church. The Septuagint is the pre-Christian Greek version of Jewish Scriptures.

We have all probably at one time planted a beautiful flower garden only to have it choked with weeds and grass, so we can empathize with God when God made this statement in 2 Esdras,[23] Greek for Ezra, in the Apocrypha:

> *19) ..... I looked at my world, and there it lay spoilt, at my earth (20) in danger from men's wicked thoughts; and at the sight I could scarcely (21) bring myself to spare them. One grape I saved out of a cluster .....(2 Esdras 9:19-21, The Apocrypha.)*

We know that grape to be Israel. Now, with the first coming of Christ and the Age of Grace, the Jews are still God's chosen people, but they have been set aside for a time until the fulness of the time of the Gentiles (Luke 21:24; Romans 11:25) which is throughout the entire period of the Age of Grace. Gentiles who have been adopted into the family of Israel by salvation through Jesus Christ are also set apart for the same primary purpose, to serve and worship God. Knowing the eternal benefits God offers makes it a privilege to serve rather than a hardship.

The question is asked countless times: What about the Jew of today whose religion is still Judaism, believing that their Messiah is yet to come? Are they all lost? Paul explains:

> *Isaiah the prophet cried out concerning the Jews that though there would be millions of them, only a small number of them would be saved.....(Romans 9:27.)*

Is this fair? Paul also settles the question of God's fairness to the Jew and also answers many questions pertaining to the Jews of today:

> *(6) Well then, has God failed to fulfill his promises to the Jews? No! For those promises are only to those who are truly Jews. And not everyone born into a Jewish family is truly a Jew! (7) Just the fact that they come from Abraham doesn't make them truly Abraham's children.*

> *For the Scriptures say that the promises apply only to Abraham's son Isaac and Isaac's descendants, though Abraham had other children too. (8) This means that not all of Abraham's children are children of God, but only those who believe the promise of salvation which he made to Abraham.*

> *(9) For God had promised, "Next year I will give you and Sarah a son." (10-13) And years later, when this son Isaac was grown up and married and Rebecca his wife was about to bear him twin children, God told her that Esau, the child born first, would be a servant to Jacob, his twin brother.*

> *In the words of the Scripture, "I chose to bless Jacob, but not Esau." And God said this before the children were even born, before they had done anything either good or bad. This proves that God was doing what he had decided from the beginning; it was not because of what the children did but because of what God wanted and chose.*

(14) Was God being unfair? Of course not. (15) For God had said to Moses, "If I want to be kind to someone, I will. And I will take pity on anyone I want to." (16) And so God's blessings are not given just because someone decides to have them or works hard to get them. They are given because God takes pity on those he wants to.

(17) Pharaoh, the King of Egypt, was an example of this fact. For God told him he had given him the kingdom of Egypt for the very purpose of displaying the awesome power of God against him so that all the world would hear about God's glorious name. (18) So you see, God is kind to some just because he wants to be, and he makes some refuse to listen. (19) Well then, why does God blame them for not listening? Haven't they done what he made them do?

(20) No, don't say that. Who are you to criticize God? Should the thing made say to the one who made it, "Why have you made me like this?" (21) When a man makes a jar out of clay, doesn't he have a right to use the same lump of clay to make one jar beautiful, to be used for holding flowers, and another to throw garbage into?

(22) Does not God have a perfect right to show his fury and power against those who are fit only for destruction, those he has been patient with for all this time? (23-24) And he has a right to take others such as ourselves, who have been made for pouring the riches of his glory into, whether we are Jews or Gentiles, and to be kind to us so that everyone can see how very great his glory is. (Romans 9:6-24.)

And Paul explains further about God's fairness to the Jews:

(18) But what about the Jews? Have they heard God's Word? Yes, for it has gone wherever they are; the Good News has been told to the ends of the earth. (19) And did

they understand [that God would give his salvation to others if they refused to take it]? Yes, for even back in the time of Moses, God had said that he would make his people jealous and try to wake them up by giving his salvation to the foolish heathen nations. (Romans 10:18-19.)

This is Paul's answer to the following question:

I ask then, has God rejected and deserted his people the Jews? Oh no, not at all. Remember that I myself am a Jew, a descendant of Abraham and a member of Benjamin's family. (Romans 11:1.)

And Paul continues to explain:

(7) So this is the situation: Most of the Jews have not found the favor of God they are looking for. A few have--the ones God has picked out--but the eyes of the others have been blinded. (8) This is what our Scriptures refer to when they say that God has put them to sleep, shutting their eyes and ears so that they do not understand what we are talking about when we tell them of Christ. And so it is to this very day. (Romans 11:7-8.)

(11) Does this mean that God has rejected his Jewish people forever? Of course not! His purpose was to make his salvation available to the Gentiles, and then the Jews would be jealous and begin to want God's salvation for themselves.

(12) Now if the whole world became rich as a result of God's offer of salvation, when the Jews stumbled over it and turned it down, think how much greater a blessing the world will share in later on when the Jews, too, come to Christ. (Romans 11:11-12.)

And last, Paul gives this hope for the Jews:

(25) I want you to know about this truth from God, dear brothers, so that you will not feel proud and start bragging. Yes, it is true that some of the Jews have set themselves against the Gospel now, but this will last only until all of you Gentiles have come to Christ--those of you who will. (26) And then all Israel will be saved. (Romans 11:25-26.)

It is only during this Twenty First Century that we see this long harsh punishment of Israel drawing to a close. In 1948 Israel was declared a state by world powers and Jews subsequently began migrating en masse back to Israel. This was the beginning of the fulfillment of the following prophecy:

(16) But tell the exiles that the Lord God says: "Although I have scattered you in the countries of the world, yet I will be a sanctuary to you for the time that you are there, (17) and I will gather you back from the nations where you are scattered and give you the land of Israel again." (Ezekiel 11:16-17.)

Then there is this further prophecy concerning Israel during the Millennium:

(14) Despised though you are, fear not, O Israel, for I will help you. I am the Lord, your Redeemer; I am the Holy One of Israel. (15) You shall be a new and sharp-toothed thrashing instrument to tear all enemies apart, making chaff of mountains. (16) You shall toss them in the air; the wind shall blow them all away; whirlwinds shall scatter them. And the joy of the Lord shall fill you full; you shall glory in the God of Israel. (Isaiah 41:14-16.)

And Amos also gives this prophecy concerning Israel during the Millennium:

I will restore the fortunes of my people Israel, and they shall rebuild their ruined cities, and live in them again, and they shall plant vineyards and gardens and eat their crops and drink their wine. (Amos 9:14.)

Hosea gives this prophecy that the Israel of long ago (the Northern Kingdom) and Judah (the Southern Kingdom) will once again be reunited and become one nation during the Millennium:

(10) Yet the time will come when Israel shall prosper and become a great nation; in that day her people will be too numerous to count--like sand along a seashore! Then instead of saying to them, "You are not my people," I will tell them, "You are my sons, children of the Living God."

11) Then the people of Judah and Israel will unite and have one leader; they will return from exile together; what a day that will be--the day when God will sow his people in the fertile soil of their own land again. (Hosea 1:10-11.)

But what is Israel's land? The Land of Canaan became the Promised Land when it was given to the Israelites by God. The boundaries of the Promised Land are designated in Joshua:

All the way from Negeb desert in the south to the Lebanon mountains in the north, and from the Mediterranean Sea in the west to the Euphrates River in the east, including all the land of the Hittites. (Joshua 1:4.)

History relating to Israel's land begins back in the days of **Noah**. Noah was 950 years old when he died (Genesis 9:29). At age 480, he was instructed by God to build an ark because God was going to flood the earth and destroy wicked mankind thereby perfecting a total cleansing of the world (Genesis 6:12-22). God gave mankind 120 years to repent (Genesis 6:3), the time in which it took Noah to build the ark. Noah was 600 years old when The Flood came and covered the earth (Genesis 7:6).

Water poured not only from the sky but also subterranean waters burst forth for forty days and nights (Genesis 7:12) and water covered the earth for 150 days (Genesis 7:24) before it began to recede. Only Noah and his wife, his three sons **Shem, Ham, Japheth** and their wives, and pairs of every kind of animals, reptiles and birds were saved (Genesis 7:13-15).

Noah became a farmer and made wine after The Flood. But because his youngest son Ham committed the indecent act of looking upon his father while he was lying naked in his tent in a drunken stupor, Noah cursed Ham's descendants. While Noah blessed Shem and Japheth, he cursed the descendants of Ham's son Canaan and decreed that they were to become slaves to Shem and Japheth and their descendants (Genesis 9:20-25). Scripture does not enlighten us as to why it was Canaan Noah chose to curse.

The *Hittites*[24] were the descendants of Canaan's second son Heth and occupied what today is central Turkey and extended into Palestine. Some of them later moved into the land of Canaan. They were one of the three great powers of that time, but Noah's curse followed them. The Canaanites were dispossessed when the twelve tribes originating from the twelve sons of Jacob took possession of the Promised Land under the leadership of Joshua about 1406 B.C.

The *Philistines*, were also dispossessed when the Israelites took possession of the Promised Land. They were a sea people from the Greek Islands, probably Crete, having failed in their invasion of Egypt, invaded and occupied what is now Palestine. Our word Palestine is derived from the term Philistine, and the Jews holy city Jerusalem is located in Palestine.

More important history pertaining to Israel and the Promised Land of the Jews[25] is the following:

Muhammad became acquainted with the Old and New Testament and wanted to be identified with the holy city Jerusalem. So Jerusalem is important to Muslims, Christians, and Jews. It is important to the Muslims because they are taught that Muhammad was miraculously carried to Jerusalem and consecrated there. It is

THE TRAGEDY OF ISRAEL

important to the Jews because it is their holy city. It is important to the Christians because of Christ.

In 614, a Persian general seized Jerusalem slaughtering 60,000 Christians and took 35,000 as slaves. The first Dome of the Rock (Muslim temple) was erected in 688 on the site of Israel's destroyed Temple. In 1099, Jerusalem was again seized by the Christians, but the shameful, unnecessary, and terrible slaughter of Muslims by the Christian Army of the First Crusade has not been forgiven nor forgotten by the Muslims.

To the shame of the Christian world, the great Saladin, in 1187, after his victorious battle with the Crusaders at the Horns of Hattin captured Jerusalem without violence.

General Allenby of the British forces entered Jerusalem on December 9, 1917, and an armistice was signed on October 31, 1918, ending 400 years of the rule of the Ottoman Turks Empire. On April 24, 1920, a mandate for Palestine and Transjordan was assigned to Great Britain. Then on May 14, 1948, this mandate was terminated, and the National Council at Tel-Aviv declared Israel a state.

A nation was reborn in the Promised Land of the Jews, and the following prophecies of Amos and Hosea were fulfilled. This is the prophecy of Amos:

> *"I will firmly plant them there upon the land that I have given them; they shall not be pulled up again," says the Lord your God. (Amos 9:15.)*

And this is the prophecy of Hosea:

> *After two days he will revive us; in the third day he will raise us up, and we shall live in his sight. (Hosea 6:2 KJV.)*

The final restoration of Israel was begun. Hosea's prophecy is right on target timewise with present day events. Hosea lived in the 500s B.C. Two days have passed. How do we know? Hosea said after two days and sometime in the third day, Israel would be revived and raised up. Israel has been **revived and raised up** (barely). But sometime within this third day Israel is to be fully restored and live in Christ's sight, according to this prophecy. This would be during the Millennium.

We are now seeing the signs described in Matthew 24:7-8 of wars with Israel, wars and rumors of wars, famines, earthquakes, floods, and changing weather patterns worldwide that are the beginning of the birth pangs that herald in the holocausts that immediately precede the Millennium.

For years, the Jews have been fighting to regain their holy city Jerusalem and regain possession of their Promised Land. Primetime or 60 Minutes or some such documentary in the latter part of 1992 presented a program in which some Palestinians were being interviewed. The interviewee was a middle-aged woman who, in essence, said we have spent all our lives building our homes here and accumulating what possessions we have. This has been our land for hundreds of years. Now the Jews say: God gave us this land; we want it; you give it to us. To give up our land means the loss of everything we have.

Naturally, they do not want to give up their homes and their land, nor would we if we were in the same situation, but God decreed the land long ago to be Israel's. Therefore, they might as well give it to them because, according to prophecy, it will be Israel's in the end. The human side though is that our heart goes out to those who have been dispossessed because it would be the same as someone coming in and telling us we must vacate our homes and lands because it was theirs.

Thousand upon thousands of people have become refugees as seen in news broadcasts, lost their homes and their land. They are simply victims of their time, living on lands their ancestors conquered hundreds of years ago.

Today as we are in this year of 2004, the conflict between the Jews and Muslims continues and is constantly in the news. The Jews are still fighting for their land. I believe that if those fighting against Israel today would study Israel's history and prophecies, they would literally lay down their arms because they would know they cannot win. God has said it, *"They shall not be pulled up again." (Amos 9:15.)*

THE TRAGEDY OF ISRAEL

The tragedy of Israel is that they didn't have to be pulled up from their land and have their nation destroyed; they didn't have to be scattered all over the world; and they didn't have to suffer those hundreds and hundreds of years of persecution. If they had just worshiped the Lord their God and kept his commandments, they could have continued as a continuous dynasty, being blessed as a nation of God's chosen people all those years as promised to King David.

Weep for the Jew; the worst is yet to come. The prophecy is that God again divides Israel into three parts, two parts to be destroyed, but this time instead of scattering the last one-third into all nations, they are to be purified.

Two-thirds of all the Nation of Israel will be cut off and die, but a third will be left in the land. I will bring the third that remain through the fire and make them pure, as gold and silver are refined and purified by fire. (Zechariah 13:8.)

This corresponds with the prophecy which states that during the end times of the tribulation, *Many shall be purified by great trials and persecutions....(Daniel 12:10.)*

Weep for the Jew as time relentlessly and inexorably moves toward the last and final terrible punishment of Israel, the holocausts of the Great Tribulation during the reign of the Anti-Christ and False Prophet.

CHAPTER 5
WHO ARE THE ANTI-CHRIST AND FALSE PROPHET

The prophecy is that the Anti-Christ will be a world ruler, empowered by Satan, during the end times and the tribulation period. The False Prophet is a religious leader who leads the world populace into a false religion during the reign of the Anti-Christ. We know who Satan is that empowers the Anti-Christ:

> *This great Dragon--the ancient serpent called the devil, or Satan, the one deceiving the whole world--was thrown down onto the earth with all his army. (Revelation 12:9.)*

The prophecies relating to these two personages are very difficult to understand because they are written in apocalyptic language (signs and symbols) referring to beasts, animals, heads, horns, kings, and crowns.

The prophecies of Daniel in the Old Testament and John on the Island of Patmos in the Book of Revelation helps in learning the true meaning of who the coming Evil Creature (Anti-Christ) and the False Prophet are. It is believed that John who was exiled to the Island of Patmos was the disciple of Christ. As stated before, the prophet Daniel was born about 621 B.C. and was in one of the first groups of hostages King Nebuchadnezzar took to Babylon in 605 B.C. when he first conquered Judah.

The last six chapters of the Book of Daniel gives Daniel's prophecies of the end times. Daniel gives three different prophecies of the ten world powers that are to come out of which the Anti-Christ is to rise:

> *(2) In my dream I saw a great storm on a mighty ocean with strong winds blowing from every direction. (3) Then four huge animals came up out of the water, each different from the other.*

(4) The first was like a lion, but it had eagle's wings! And as I watched, its wings were pulled off so that it could no longer fly, and it was left standing on the ground, on two feet, like a man, and a man's mind was given to it.

(5) The second animal looked like a bear with its paw raised, ready to strike. It held three ribs between its teeth, and I heard a voice saying to it. "Get up! Devour many people!"

(6) The third of these strange animals looked like a leopard, but on its back it had wings like those of birds, and it had four heads! And great power was given to it over all mankind.

(7) Then, as I watched in my dream, a fourth animal rose up out of the ocean, too dreadful to describe and incredibly strong. It devoured some of its victims by tearing them apart with its huge iron teeth, and others it crushed beneath its feet. It was far more brutal and vicious than any of the other animals, and it had ten horns. (Daniel 7:2-7.)

This is the explanation of the above prophecy:

(15) I was confused and disturbed by all I had seen (Daniel wrote in his report), (16) so I approached one of those standing beside the throne and asked him the meaning of all these things, and he explained them to me. (17) "These four huge animals," he said, "represent four kings who will someday rule the earth. (18) But in the end, the people of the Most High God shall rule the governments of the world forever and forever." (Daniel 7:15-18.)

Very simply stated, the prophetic symbolic animals that rise out of the ocean or sea, meaning masses of people (Revelation 17:15), represent empires or kings that rose to world power and have fallen, or are yet to rise to world power.

Counting the four world powers that have fallen, it is believed that the first animal (world power, the lion) was Babylon. Then the second animal (world power, the bear) Medo-Persia. The third animal (world power, the leopard) Greece, led by Alexander the Great.[26] This conquering hero died of a fever in 323 B.C. at the age of 32, and his vast empire was divided among four of his generals. This then would represent the four heads of the third animal. The fourth animal, the most vicious and brutal world power with the ten horns, would represent the Great Roman Empire:

(19) Then I asked about the fourth animal, the one so brutal and shocking, with its iron teeth and brass claws that tore men apart and that stamped others to death with its feet. (20) I asked, too, about the ten horns and the little horn that came up afterward and destroyed three of the others--the horn with the eyes and the loud bragging mouth, the one which was stronger than the others. (21) For I had seen this horn warring against God's people and winning, (22) until the Ancient of Days came and opened his court and vindicated his people, giving them worldwide powers of government.

(23) "This fourth animal," he told me, "is the fourth world power that will rule the earth. It will be more brutal than any of the others. It will devour the whole world, destroying everything before it. (24) His ten horns are ten kings that will rise out of his empire. Then another king will arise, more brutal than the other ten, and will destroy three of them. (25) He will defy the Most High God, and wear down the saints with persecutions, and try to change all laws, morals, and customs. God's people will be helpless in his hands for three and a half years." (Daniel 7:19-25.)

The Great Roman Empire fell hundreds of years ago, but the ten horns of this brutal and vicious beast, the fourth world power, represent ten leaders of ten countries that will rise out of what was the Roman Empire. The king that rises with the loud bragging mouth, of course, represents the Anti-Christ, and he destroys three of the ten kings or leaders. He wars against and defeats God's people and becomes a world ruler over all nations (Revelation 13:7).

The next prophecy of Daniel is worded differently but means the same thing:

(1) In the third year of the reign of King Belshazzar, I had another dream similar to the first. (2) This time I was at Susa, the capital in the province of Elam, standing beside the Ulai River. (3) As I was looking around, I saw a ram with two long horns standing on the river bank; and as I watched, one of these horns began to grow, so that it was longer than the other. (4) The ram butted everything out of its way and no one could stand against it or help its victims. It did as it pleased and became very great.

(5) While I was wondering what this could mean, suddenly a buck goat appeared from the west, so swiftly that it didn't even touch the ground. This goat, which had one very large horn between its eyes, (6) rushed furiously at the two-horned ram. (7) And the closer he came, the angrier he was. He charged into the ram and broke off both his horns. Now the ram was helpless and the buck goat knocked him down and trampled him, for there was no one to rescue him. (8) The victor became both proud and powerful, but suddenly, at the height of his power, his horn was broken, and in its place grew four good-sized horns pointing in four directions. (Daniel 8:1-8.)

Again, this prophecy is explained. The ram would represent the Medo-Persian Empire. The goat would represent the Grecian Empire. The great Grecian Empire also fell, and the four horns would represent the division of the Grecian Empire to the four generals of Alexander the Great. And none of the generals that rose to power in the division of the Grecian Empire were as great as Alexander the Great. This is the explanation:

(19) "I am here," he said, "to tell you what is going to happen in the last days of the coming time of terror--for what you have seen pertains to that final event in history. (20) The two horns of the ram you saw are the kings of Media and Persia; (21) the shaggy-haired goat is the nation of Greece, and its long horn represents the first great king of that country. (22) When you saw the horn break off, the four smaller horns replace it, this meant that the Grecian Empire will break into four sections with four kings, none of them as great as the first." (Daniel 8:19-22.)

Then Daniel begins to describe **not** the Great Roman Empire that conquered Greece but the ten world powers that are to rise during the end times out of what was the Roman Empire and the rise of the Anti-Christ:

(23) "Toward the end of their kingdoms, when they have become morally rotten, an angry king shall rise to power with great shrewdness and intelligence. (24) His power shall be mighty, but it will be satanic strength and not his own. Prospering wherever he turns, he will destroy all who oppose him, though their armies be mighty, and he will devastate God's people.

(25) He will be a master of deception, defeating many by catching them off guard as they bask in false security. Without warning he will destroy them. So great will he fancy himself to be that he will even take on the Prince of Princes in battle; but in so doing he will seal his own doom, for he shall be broken by the hand of God, though no human means could overpower him. (Daniel 8:23-25.)

Th other prophecy of Daniel is of the powerful statute of a man with the head of gold that represents Babylon; the chest and arms of silver that represent Medo-Persia; the belly and thighs of brass that represent Greece, and the legs of iron with feet of iron and clay with ten toes represent the Roman Empire. The feet of part iron and part clay with the ten toes represent the ten countries that will rise to power in the end times out of what was the Roman Empire (Daniel 2:37-43).

The above three prophecies of Daniel of the rise of the Anti-Christ correspond to the Book of Revelation which was written hundreds of years after Daniel's prophecies by John on the Island of Patmos:

> *(1) And now, in my vision, I saw a strange Creature rising up out of the sea. It had seven heads and ten horns, and ten crown upon its horns ....(Revelation 13:1.)*

And the meaning of these seven heads is explained:

> *(9) And now think hard. His seven heads represent a certain city built on seven hills where this woman has her residence. (10) They also represent seven kings. Five have already fallen, the sixth now reigns, and the seventh is yet to come, but his reign will be brief. (Revelation 17:9-10.)*

The city represents Rome on her seven hills. Six of the kings that ruled the Roman Empire have already fallen, died. This seventh king represented by the seventh head yet to come is the leader who will rise and eventually become the Anti-Christ. This leader, the Anti-Christ, dies but is miraculously brought back to life by the power of Satan. His death and how he was healed is also described:

> *I saw that one of his heads seemed wounded beyond recovery-- but the fatal wound was healed! All the world marveled at this miracle and followed the Creature in awe. (Revelation 13:3.)*

Now, the creature with the seven heads also has ten horns, and these horns have crowns representing the same ten kings or world leaders of Daniel's prophecies which are to rise out of the Old Roman Empire. They are be the pawns of the Anti-Christ:

> *His ten horns are ten kings who have not yet risen to power; they will be appointed to their kingdoms for one brief moment to reign with him. (Revelation 17:12.)*

After the miraculous recovery from death of the seventh head (king), he appears among the ten leaders as the Anti-Christ. These ten leaders will sign a treaty giving their power and strength to the Anti-Christ (Revelation 17:13). He will then destroy three of the ten countries represented by the ten horns.

> *As I was looking at the horns, suddenly another small horn appeared among them, and three of the first ones were yanked out, roots and all, to give it room; this little horn had a man's eyes and a bragging mouth. (Daniel 7:8.)*

This personage represented by the small horn who appears among the ten horns is the leader who was the seventh head of Revelation 13:7, the Anti-Christ who died and was brought back to life. The Anti-Christ then becomes the eighth king or world ruler who is also referred to as the scarlet animal:

> *The scarlet animal that died is the eighth king, having reigned before as one of the seven; after his second reign, he too, will go to his doom. (Revelation 17:11.)*

Thus begins the reign of the Anti-Christ. Many will believe the Anti-Christ to be the Messiah and that Christ has returned because of the miracles he is able to perform by the power given him by Satan. Empowered by Satan, called the Dragon, the Anti-Christ will rule the whole world. Unbelievable? Yes. But listen to this!

> *(7) The Dragon gave him power to fight against God's people and to overcome them, and to rule over all nations and language groups throughout the world. (8) And all mankind--whose names were not written down before the*

founding of the world in the slain Lamb's Book of Life--worshiped the evil Creature. (Revelation 13:7-8.)

Now, **who is the False Prophet?** This picturesque description is given:

(11) Then I saw another strange animal, this one coming up out of the earth, with two little horns like those of a lamb but a fearsome voice like the Dragon's. (12) He exercised all the authority of the Creature whose death-wound had been headed, whom he required all the world to worship. (13) He did unbelievable miracles such as making fire flame down to earth from the skies while everyone was watching.

(14) By doing these miracles, he was deceiving people everywhere. He could do these marvelous things whenever the first Creature was there to watch him. And he ordered the people of the world to make a great statue of the first Creature, who was fatally wounded and then came back to life. (15) He was permitted to give breath to this statue and even make it speak! Then the statue ordered that anyone refusing to worship it must die!

16) He required everyone--great and small, rich and poor, slave and free--to be tattooed with a certain mark on the right hand or on the forehead. (17) And no one could get a job or even buy in any store without the permit of that mark, which was either the name of the Creature or the code number of his name. (18) Here is a puzzle that calls for careful thought to solve. Let those who are able, interpret this code: The numerical values of the letters in his name add to 666!. (Revelation 13:11-18.)

Hal Lindsey, in his book *There's a New World Coming,*[27] sheds some light on the meaning of who this strange animal represents. This animal comes from the earth, symbolizing land belonging to Israel.

He is probably a Jew. He has two horns but no crown; therefore, he is not a king or political power but a religious leader. He is like a lamb symbolizing that he will imitate the real Lamb Jesus Christ and will have great power given to him by the Evil Creature (Anti-Christ). He will organize a world-wide religious system into a false religion, a religion that deceives many into believing that the Anti-Christ is the Messiah returned because of the miracles he is able to perform. Therefore, he is called the False Prophet.

The False Prophet is also referred to as the Notorious Prostitute.

> *One of the seven angels who had poured out the plaques came over and talked with me. "Come with me," he said, "and I will show you what is going to happen to the Notorious Prostitute, who sits upon the many waters of the world." (Revelation 17:1.)*

And the many waters of the world that the Notorious Prostitute sits upon is explained and confirms his religious control, along with the Anti-Christ, over people worldwide:

> *"The oceans, lakes and rivers that the woman is sitting on represent masses of people of every race and nation." (Revelation 17:15.)*

With these many miraculous feats performed by the False Prophet, **how can the unsuspecting populace know that the Anti-Christ is not the real Messiah Christ?** Very simple! The Anti-Christ comes from the nations of the earth and its masses of people. When Christ comes again**,** he will come in the clouds, just as he left (Acts 1:11). There will be no doubt whatsoever:

> *For when I return, you will know it beyond all doubt. It will be as evident as the lightning that flashes across the skies. (Luke 17:24.)*

Also, the rise of the Anti-Christ and the False Prophet precedes the return of the real Messiah Christ. Be ever watchful so as not to be deceived (Matthew 24:24) by the supernatural power given to the Anti-Christ by Satan and the great deception he and the False Prophet perpetrate upon the whole world. Beware of the coming of the Anti-Christ and the False Prophet! The rise of the Anti-Christ heralds in the seven-year period of the prophecy in Daniel 9:27 and the Great Tribulation!

CHAPTER 6

THE GREAT TRIBULATION

A study of the second and third chapters of the Book of Revelation concerning the letters written to the seven churches, which are compared to the churches of the ages and of today, reveals an enlightening fact in God's messages concerning not just the Jew but the Church, Christians, pertaining to the Great Tribulation.

To the church in Philadelphia (the sixth church), the message is very good in that they are praised and given this assurance:

Because you have patiently obeyed me despite the persecution, therefore I will protect you from the time of the Great Tribulation and temptation which will come upon the world to test everyone that is alive. (Revelation 3:10)

This is the only one of the seven churches that has been promised that they will be exempt from the Great Tribulation. Why? Why would there be a need to tell this particular church that they would be spared? What about the first five churches? We can only speculate that the first five were obviously so far removed in time that there was no need to reassure them, but this church in Philadelphia, being next to the last church would need this reassurance because they were so close to the time when the tribulation would take place.

But what about the message to the church in Laodicea (the seventh church)? There is no such reassurance that they will escape the Great Tribulation. Listen to the warning to this seventh and last church, and the church age of today:

(14) "Write this letter to the leader of the church in Laodicea: This message is from the one who stand firm, the faithful and true witness [of all that is or was or evermore shall be] the primeval source of God's creation. (15) I know you well. You are neither hot nor cold. I wish you were one or the other. (16) But since you are merely lukewarm, I will spit you out of my mouth.

(17) You say, 'I am rich, with everything I want; I don't need a thing.' And you don't realize that spiritually you are wretched and miserable and poor and blind and naked. (18) My advice to you is to buy pure gold from me, gold purified by fire. Only then will you truly be rich. And to purchase from me white garments, white and pure, so you won't be naked and ashamed, and to get medicine from me to heal your eyes and give you back your sight. (19) I continually discipline and punish everyone I love so I must punish you unless you turn from your indifference and become enthusiastic about the things of God.

20) Look, I have been standing at the door and I am constantly knocking. If anyone hears me calling him and opens the door, I will come in and fellowship with him and he with me. (21) I will let everyone who conquers sit beside me on my throne, just as I took my place with my Father on his throne when I had conquered. (22) Let those who can hear listen to what the Spirit is saying to the churches." (Revelation 3:14-22.)

What does this message mean to us? Simply this:

First, today, we are lukewarm and lack zeal in spreading the Gospel when the opportunity arises (Revelation 3:15).

Second, we are blessed with much materially but are spiritually poor because we put the things of the world before God (Revelation 3:17).

Third, we fail to do enough good works that will be counted as gold that will withstand the test of fire. (1 Corinthians 3:13; Revelation 3:18.)

Fourth, even in the churches, many fail to purchase white garments which means to accept salvation by believing in Christ, repenting of sins, and making Christ Lord of their life by living by his laws. Instead of going to church for the primary purpose of worshiping God, church becomes a social event.

Fifth, to conquer means to endure persecution; that is, declare boldly we are Christians in the face of ridicule or physical persecution, even unto the death. The rewards will be great. Christ will let us sit beside him on his throne (Revelation 3:21).

And, sixth, every person who is alive during the tribulation will be tested as to his faith in Jesus Christ (Revelation 3:10; 13:9-10). As Christians, we should all ask this question: Could I withstand this test? Is my faith strong enough to enable me to die for Christ? If it isn't, we need to do some real soul searching.

John, exiled on the Island of Patmos describes his vision as God revealed a detailed picture of the Great Tribulation, the Rapture, the Second Coming of Christ, the Wrath of God, and man's final destiny throughout all eternity. This is what John saw:

> *Then as I looked, I saw a door standing open in heaven, and the same voice I had heard before, that sounded like a mighty trumpet blast, spoke to me and said, "Come up here and I will show you what must happen in the future!" (Revelation 4:1.)*

Notice that it is the future, not the past or the present of John's time that John will see. As the very end times of the world are revealed to John, the prophecy that states the length of time for these events is the seven-year period which will usher in the reign of the Anti-Christ:

> *This king will make a seven-year treaty with the people, but after half that time, he will break his pledge.....(Daniel 9:27.)*

This seven-year period is divided into two three-and-a-half year periods:

1. The first three-and-a-half year period ushers in world peace during the reign of the world leader, the Anti-Christ, with the breaking of the first Seal (Revelation 6:1-2).

2. The second three-and-a-half year period is Judgment of the World through tribulation (John 12:31), and the holocausts begin with the breaking of the second Seal (Revelation 7:3-4) and last through the blowing of the seven trumpets.

It is presumed that the pouring out of the wrath of God is included in this last three-and-a-half year period during the Judgment of the World through tribulation. However, the two powerful witnesses that are raised up in Revelation 11:3-6 are called up or resurrected after their three-and-a-half years of witnessing just prior to the blowing of the seventh trumpet (Revelation 11:12-15) strongly indicating that the last three-and-a-half years of the tribulation end with the seventh trumpet. Thus, this points out that the wrath of God which may last an indeterminate amount of time could commence at the conclusion of the entire seven-year period and continue until the Second Coming of Christ to begin the Millennium.

Judgment of the world through tribulation consists of the following:

1. The terrors during the breaking of the Seals, two through six (Revelation 6:3-17).

2. The terrors during the breaking of the seventh Seal (Revelation 8:1-5).

3. The terrors during the first four Trumpets (Revelation 8:6-12).

4. The terrors during the fifth Trumpet, the **first Woe** (Revelation 8:13; 9:1-12).

5. The terrors during the sixth Trumpet, the **second Woe** (Revelation 9:13-21).

6. The Seven Thunders speak (Revelation 10:3-4).

7. The terrors of the seventh Trumpet: Christ takes control of the world (Revelation 11:15). The **third Woe.** The Rapture (Revelation 10:7, 11:14-17, Matthew 24:30-31, 1 Corinthians 15:52, Mark 13:24-27, Luke 21:27-28). The judgments of mankind begins (Revelation 11:18).

Daniel confirms the length of these terrors are to last three-and-a-half years after the power of God's people has been crushed. And the power of God's people is crushed when the Anti-Christ breaks his treaty at the beginning of the second three-and-a-half years.

(4) But Daniel, keep this prophecy a secret; seal it up so that it will not be understood until the end times when education

and travel shall be vastly increased." (5) Then I, Daniel, looked and saw two men on each bank of a river. (6) And one of them asked the man in linen robes who was standing now above the river, "How long will it be until all these terrors end?" (7) He replied, with both hands lifted to heaven, taking oath by him who lives forever and ever, that they will not end until three-and-a-half years after the power of God's people has been crushed. (Daniel 12:4-7.)

It is only during these end times that these prophecies are beginning to be understood. Why did God tell Daniel to keep this prophecy a secret? God did not reveal the reason. But as the end time approaches those affected need to be prepared for what is coming.

How near is that time? We don't know, but never in history has there been so much travel, including world travel. The airports are usually full. Nor has there ever been so much knowledge and education. Since late in the 18th Century, the world has experienced the Industrial Revolution with the ever-expanding introduction of machines, including the locomotive, automobile, and airplane.

We live today in the Twentieth First Century in an age of miracle drugs and modern medical science, the atomic and space age, and now world events reflect the groundwork being laid for the Anti-Christ's ability to control the whole world through the economy system in this ever-expanding computer age. Compared to thousands of prior years, this is a vast increase in knowledge in a very short period of time.

The age-old question is still being asked: When will all these things happen? When will the Tribulation occur? When will the Rapture occur? When will Christ return to set up his kingdom? Even the disciples asked Christ what the sign of his coming and the end of this age would be:

"When will this happen?" the disciples asked him later, as he sat on the slopes of the Mount of Olives. "What events will signal your return, and the end of the world" (Matthew 24:3.)

Jesus gives the signs to look for, not when it will happen:

(4) Jesus told them, "Don't let anyone fool you. (5) For many will come claiming to be the Messiah and lead many astray. (6) When you hear of wars beginning, this does not signal my return: these must come, but the end is not yet. (7) The nations and kingdoms of the earth will rise against each other and there will be famines and earthquakes in many places. (8) But all this will be only the beginning of the horrors to come." (Matthew 24:4-8.)

Again, even after his resurrection, the disciples asked Christ if he was going to set up his kingdom at that time:

..... "Lord, are you going to free Israel now and restore us as an independent nation?" "The Father sets those dates," he replied, "and they are not for you to know." (Acts 1:6.)

And Christ further emphasizes that no one knows when he will return, except the Father:

"But no one knows the date and hour when the end will be-- not even the angels. No, nor even God's Son. Only the Father knows." (Matthew 24:36.)

It should be understood that there is a vast difference between Christ's Second Coming and the Rapture. The word Rapture is derived from the Latin word *raptus* meaning to be caught up. The term Rapture is used to distinguish between the gathering up of the Christians (the Church) in the air to meet Christ and Christ's Second Coming in which he begins his Millennium reign.

There is controversy and different concepts taught concerning *when* the Rapture occurs. One is Pre-Tribulation which teaches that the Rapture occurs prior to the entire seven-year period of the Anti-Christ's reign. One is Mid-Tribulation which teaches that the Rapture occurs after the first three-and-one-half years of peace but before the holocausts of the second three-and-a-half years begin. One is that the Rapture occurs at the blowing of the seventh trumpet. One is Post-Millennium which teaches that the Rapture occurs after the entire Millennium has ended. And another is that there is no Rapture.

Pre-tribulation teachings that the Rapture occurs prior to the seven-year period and tribulation are based partially on Scripture that Christians are to be spared the wrath of God. That the Christians are to be spared the wrath of God is confirmed in Paul's teachings:

> *For God has not chosen to pour out his wrath on us, but to save us through our Lord Jesus Christ. (1 Thessalonians 5:9.)*

However, the undiluted wrath of God is not poured out upon the world (Revelation 15:1, 16:1) until after the tribulation, after the holocausts of the seven seals and seven trumpets have occurred. This is not taken into consideration as none want to hear that Christians could be subjected to any of the horrors and trials of the holocausts.

Seventh Trumpet Rapture teachings rely on Revelation 10:7; 2 Thessalonians 2:3; and the Gospels of Mark, Luke, and Matthew indicating that the Rapture will occur at the end of the tribulation, at the end of the holocausts of the Seals and Trumpets when the seventh trumpet is blown.

The Gospel of Mark states this:

> *(24) "After the tribulation ends, then the sun will grow dim and the moon will not shine, (25) and the stars will fall-- the heavens will convulse. (26) Then all mankind will see me, the Messiah, coming in the clouds with great power and glory. (27) And I will send out the angels to gather together my chosen ones from all over the world--from the farthest bounds of earth and heaven." (Mark 13:24-27.)*

And the Gospel of Luke states this:

> *(25) "Then there will be strange events in the skies-- warnings, evil omens and portents in the sun, moon, and*

stars; and down here on earth the nations will be in turmoil, perplexed by the roaring seas and strange tides. (26) The courage of many people will falter because of the fearful fate they see coming upon the earth, for the stability of the very heavens will be broken up. (27) Then the peoples of the earth shall see me, the Messiah, coming in a cloud with power and great glory. (28) So when all these things begin to happen, stand straight and look up! For your salvation is near." Luke 21:25-28.)

Then the Gospel of Matthew states this:

(29) "Immediately after the persecution of those days the sun will be darkened, and moon will not give light, and the stars will seem to fall from the heavens, and the powers overshadowing the earth will be convulsed. (30) And then at last the signal of my coming will appear in the heavens and there will be deep mourning all around the earth. And the nations of the world will see me arrive in the clouds of heaven, with power and great glory. (31) And I shall send forth my angels with the sound of a mighty trumpet blast, and they shall gather my chosen ones from the farthest ends of the earth and heaven.

(32) Now, learn a lesson from the fig tree. When her branch is tender and the leaves begin to sprout, you know that summer is almost here. (33) Just so, when you see all these things beginning to happen, you can know that my return is near, even at the doors. (34) Then at last this age will come to its close." (Matthew 24:30-34.)

Many presume the above Scripture in Matthew relates to the Second Coming of Christ to begin his Millennium reign. However, it points out that the signal of his Second Coming to begin his Millennium reign is the nations seeing him arrive in the clouds and sending forth his angels to gather his chosen ones, the Christians, in the air (Matthew

24:31); that his Second Coming will be right on the heels of that signal and will occur within that generation (Matthew 24:32-33).

Paul also teaches that Christ will not return to begin his Millennium reign nor will we be gathered together to meet him in the air until a great rebellion against God occurs and the Anti-Christ, referred to as the son of hell, rises to power at the beginning of the seven-year period:

> *(1-2) And now what about the coming again of our Lord Jesus Christ, and our being gathered together to meet him? Please don't be upset and excited, dear brothers, by the rumor that this day of the Lord has already begun. If you hear of people having visions and special messages from God about this, or letters that are supposed to have come from me, don't believe them.*
>
> *(3) Don't be carried away and deceived regardless of what they say. For that day will not come until two things happen: First, there will be a time of great rebellion against God, and then the man of rebellion will come--the son of hell. (2 Thessalonians 2:1-3.)*

And last, the proclamation of the angel that God's veiled plan is to be fulfilled at the blowing of the seventh trumpet:

> *(7) but that when the seventh angel blew his trumpet, then God's veiled plan--mysterious through the ages ever since it was announced by his servants the prophets--would be fulfilled. (Revelation 10:7.)*

What is God's veiled plan, the mystery of the ages? Scripture points toward this mystery being the plan of salvation which is the resurrection through Jesus Christ the Lord that was announced by the prophets thousands of years ago strongly indicating the resurrection of the Christians or Rapture taking place at this time. And even though the prophets wrote about it, they did not understand it. Even the angels did not understand and wanted to know more about it (1 Peter 1:10-

12, 20). Some of these Scriptures pertaining to this mystery are listed in Mark. 4:11; Romans 11:25, 16:25; 1 Corinthians. 2: 7; Ephesians 1:4-10, 3:3-9, 5:32, 6:19; and Colossians 1:25-26, 2:2. Specifically Romans states this:

> *Now to him that is of power to establish you according to my gospel, and the preaching of Jesus Christ according to the revelation of the mystery, which was kept secret since the world began. (Romans 16:25 KJV.)*

The Living Bible words the above verse this way:

> *I commit you to God, who is able to make you strong and steady in the Lord, just as the Gospel says, and just as I have told you. This is God's plan of salvation for you Gentiles, kept secret from the beginning of time. (Romans 16:25.)*

And Ephesians continues:

> *(7) In whom we have redemption through his blood, the forgiveness of sins, according to the riches of his grace; (8) Wherein he has abounded toward us in all wisdom and prudence; (9) Having made known unto us the mystery of his will, according to his good pleasure which he hath purposed in himself; (10) That in the dispensation of the fulness of times he might gather together in one all things in Christ, both which are in heaven, and which are on earth; even in him. (Ephesians 1:7-10 KJV.)*

And finally Colossians also explains God's veiled plan, the mystery of the ages:

> *(26) Even the mystery which hath been hid from ages and from generations, but now is made manifest to his saints; (27) To whom God would make known what is the riches of the glory of this mystery among the Gentiles; which is Christ in you, the hope of glory. (Colossians 1:26-27 KJV)*

Based on all these Scriptures, I believe the Rapture occurs at the blowing of the seventh trumpet. And I believe the fallacy of the pre-tribulation teaching is that many Christians could enter the tribulation unprepared. I want my son to be prepared and him to teach his children to be prepared. Because of the on-going peace negotiations with Israel, this time may be closer than we think.

But how can anyone prepare for such holocausts that will occur during the tribulation? No one can stockpile enough supplies to prepare for the inevitable hardships imposed because all the amenities we so much take for granted today are taken away such as utilities (electricity, water, and gas), grocery stores where we so freely buy food, employment, and possibly even homes, nor can we guard against coming persecutions.

When that day comes, no one will be allowed to work or buy unless they have the mark of the Anti-Christ and face possible starvation, imprisonment, and even death. Therefore, they are left to the mercy of those willing to help them. Impossible in our world systems today? Not at all! No one can get a job even in our country without a Social Security number nor drive a car without a driver's license. We cannot prepare for such coming unthinkable atrocities; **we can only prepare to endure them.**

The Seals:

First Seal Broken: The seven-year period begins with the breaking of the Seals. The breaking of the First Seal brings world peace (Revelation 6:2). How do we know this? The white horse possibly designates peace. The rider has a bow, designating great power, but he is a master of deception (Daniel 8:25) and conquers through diplomacy evidenced by the fact that he has no arrow.

And what is the whole world clamoring for today? World peace! But when peace comes, then comes a world leader, the Anti-Christ with it! As stated before, Revelation 13:3 informs us that this world leader will be one who has been mortally wounded, but the fatal wound was healed. Empowered by Satan, he performs many miracles; and for this reason, many will think him to be the Messiah; that the Millennium has begun; and he is able to lead many astray.

In the blindness of their delusion, the populace will willingly follow him, and the people will rejoice because at last peace has seemingly been achieved lulling the populace into a false sense of security. Perhaps many Christians, being taught the concept that they will be raptured prior to its beginning, and not yet having been raptured, will not recognize this peace as the beginning of the seven-year period and the coming tribulation.

But the Christian who studies and understands these prophecies shudders because they know that when this peace is finally achieved, it is the beginning of the reign of the Anti-Christ which precedes the terrible tribulation and pouring out of the wrath of God upon the world at the end time. Again, as stated before, one can easily distinguish between the coming of the Anti-Christ and the real Messiah? The Anti-Christ comes from the masses of people, and the real Christ comes in the clouds.

In the year of 1990, the President of our United States of America stated on national television that the nation as a whole should pray for world peace because negotiations are going forward toward that end. On September 11, 1990, President Bush stated on national television for all the world to hear that negotiations between world powers are going forward that would hopefully establish *a new world order* that would ultimately lead to world peace. He said this phrase not once but three times, a new world order. I counted them. This phrase new world order mentioned by the President was referred to again in the news, twice. And again on January 29, 1991, the President used this phrase new world order twice in his State of the Union Address.

It is particularly amazing to note that in each crises, as inter-related to Israel, we are more than ever before seeing with our own eyes fulfillment of both Old Testament and New Testament prophecies of the beginning of the end time (Matthew 24:6-8). Many are pointing out that people have been saying this for decades. But what we are seeing today is that events are happening at the accelerated pace prophesied for end times.

During the 20th Century, we have had two world wars. Many small countries have been at war at various times and are at war today. Our United States of America, in addition to world wars, was involved in the Korean, Viet Nam wars and the Gulf War. Impossible as it seems, millions of people today are starving to death. Volcanic eruptions and earthquakes are becoming more and more frequent and violent, with an unprecedented number during the 20th Century and with catastrophic earthquakes predicted by geologists within the next 30 years. Floods, mud slides burying hundreds of people alive, hurricanes, and tornadoes are striking with increased frequency worldwide with devastating results. These are common events seen in the news.

What does all this have to do with Israel and the coming Great Tribulation? World events are centered around Israel. Israel is God's time clock in prophecy. Since Israel was reestablished as a state in 1948, Jews have been migrating back to Israel in small numbers, fulfilling Old Testament prophecies (Jeremiah 31:10-11; Amos 9:8). In January, 1991, it was announced in the news that two countries had lifted their ban on Jews returning to Israel and they were returning en masse. One of these countries was Russia. I did not hear the name of the other one. Another broadcast stated that many Jews want to return to Israel in spite of the danger.

World leaders do not seem to recognize that when peace in Israel comes, as it surely is coming, the Anti-Christ and the Great Tribulation come with it. Amos gives this warning:

Woe unto you that desire the day of the Lord! To what end is it for you? The day of the Lord is darkness, and not light. (Amos 5:18 KJV.)

The Living Bible states the above verse a little differently:

You say, "If only the day of the Lord were here, for then God would deliver us from all our foes." But you have no idea what you ask. For that day will not be light and prosperity, but darkness and doom! How terrible the darkness will be for you; not a ray of joy or hope will shine. (Amos 5:18.)

Second Seal Broken: With three-and-a half years remaining of the seven-year period, the world leader or ruler--the Anti-Christ breaks his treaty and turns his satanic powers on Israel. Persecution and the Great Tribulation begin:

At that time Michael, the mighty angelic prince who sands guard over your nation will stand up [and fight for you in heaven against satanic forces], and there will be a time of anguish for the Jews greater than any previous suffering in Jewish history. And yet every one of your people whose names are written in The Book will endure it. (Daniel 12:1.)

Sometime prior to the beginning of the tribulation, the Jews will build a new Temple (Revelation 11:1) and will again offer sacrifices. When the Anti-Christ breaks his treaty after the first three-and-a-half years, he will defile the newly built Jewish temple when he sets himself up to be worshiped. He will take away these sacrifices:

From the time the daily sacrifice is taken away and the Horrible Thing is set up to be worshiped, there will be 1,290 days, (12) And blessed are those who wait and remain until the 1335th day! (Daniel 12:11-12.)

He will defy every god there is, and tear down every other object of adoration and worship. He will go in and sit as God in the temple of God claiming that he himself is God. (2 Thessalonians 2:4.)

The plight of the Jews at that time is described below:

So when you see the horrible thing (told about by Daniel the prophet) standing in a holy place, (Note to the reader: You know what is meant!), then those in Judea must flee into the Judean hills. Those on their porches must not even go inside to pack before they flee. Those in the fields should not return to their homes for their clothes. (19) And woe to pregnant women and to those with babies in those days. (20) And pray that your flight will not be in winter, or on the Sabbath. (21) For there will be persecution such as the world has never before seen in all its history, and will never see again. (Matthew 24:15-21.)

People are constantly saying **if** we have nuclear war.....It is evident that nuclear war is coming. Persecution and devastation become so great that if God does not intervene, mankind will annihilate himself; all mankind will perish:

"In fact, unless those days are shortened, all mankind will perish. But they will be shortened for the sake of God's chosen people." (Matthew 24:22.)

When the treaty is broken, peace is banished; anarchy comes to the earth; war and killing break out everywhere (Revelation 6:3-4). The Dragon in the Scripture below is Satan, and the Creature is the Anti-Christ. The Anti-Christ defeats God's people. They are persecuted, arrested, and many are killed:

(5) Then the Dragon encouraged the Creature to speak great blasphemies against the Lord; and gave him authority to control the earth for forty-two months. (6) All that time he blasphemed God's Name and his temple and all those living in heaven. (7) The Dragon gave him power to fight against God's people and to overcome them, and to rule over all nations and language groups throughout the world. (8) And all mankind--whose names were not written down before the founding of the world in the slain Lamb's Book of Life--worshiped the evil Creature.

(9) Anyone who can hear, listen carefully. (10) The people of God who are destined for prison will be arrested and taken away; those destined for death will be killed. But do not be

dismayed, for here is your opportunity for endurance and confidence. (Revelation 13:5-10.)

This description is given of how the arrests and executions are carried out with bodies left for the vultures:

(34) "That night two men will be asleep in the same room, and one will be taken away, the other left. (35,36) Two women will be working together at household tasks; one will be taken, the other left; and so it will be with men working side by side in the fields." (37) "Lord, where will they be taken?" the disciples asked. Jesus replied, "Where the body is, the vultures gather!"' (Luke 17:34-37.)

The change from peace is going to be sudden, abrupt, and without warning. Christians should not be in the dark (uniformed) about these things so that they will not be surprised when they begin to happen. Christians need to be alert and ever watchful:

(3) When people are saying, "All is well, everything is quiet and peaceful"--then, of a sudden, disaster will fall upon them as suddenly as a woman's birth pains begin when her child is born. And these people will not be able to get away anywhere--there will be no place to hide. (4) But, dear brothers, you are not in the dark about these things, and you won't be surprised as by a thief when that day of the Lord comes. (1 Thessalonians 5:3-4.)

Third Seal Broken: There is famine (Revelation 6:5).
Fourth Seal Broken: There is death, war, disease, and wild animals until **one-fourth** of the world populace is killed (Revelation 6:7-8) fulfilling an Old Testament prophecy of Ezekiel:

(16) I will shower you with deadly arrows of famine to destroy you. The famine will become more and more serious until every bit of bread is gone. (17) And not only famine

will come, but wild animals will attack you and kill you and your families; disease and war will stalk your land, and the sword of the enemy will destroy you; I, the Lord have spoken it. (Ezekiel 5:16-17.)

Fifth Seal Broken: Jesus warns his disciples and followers of what to expect:

"You will be tortured and killed and hated all over the world because you are mine." (Matthew 24:9.)

Compare the above with the following in Revelation:

(9) And when he broke open the Fifth Seal, I saw an altar and underneath it all the souls of those who had been martyred for preaching the Word of God and for being faithful in their witnessing. (10) They called loudly to the Lord and said. "O Sovereign Lord, holy and true, how long will it be before you judge the people of the earth for what they have done to us? When will you avenge our blood against those living on the earth?" (11) White robes were given to each of them and they were told to rest a little longer until their other brothers, fellow servants, had been martyred and joined them. (Revelation 6:9-11)

When the Fifth Seal is broken, those martyred throughout the ages for preaching and witnessing for God are depicted crying out to be avenged, but they are told they have to wait until the required number of fellow servants have been martyred and join them. Revelation 20:4 states the manner of these future executions, beheaded, assumed by the guillotine. How many are to be martyred during the tribulation? Not just a few, but a number too great to count:

(9) After this I saw a vast crowd, too great to count, from all nations and provinces and languages, standing in front of

the throne and before the Lamb, clothed in white, with palm branches in their hands. (10) And they were shouting with a mighty shout, "Salvation comes from our God upon the throne, and from the Lamb."

(11) And now all the angels were crowded around the throne and around the Elders and the four Living Beings, and falling face down before the throne and worshiping God. (12) "Amen," they said, "Blessing, and glory, and wisdom, and thanksgiving, and honor, and power, and might, be to our God forever and forever. Amen."

(13) Then one of the twenty-four elders asked me, "Do you know who these are, who are clothed in white, and where they come from?" (14) "No, sir," I replied. "Please tell me." "These are the ones coming out of the Great Tribulation," he said, "they washed their robes and whitened them by the blood of the Lamb." (Revelation 7:9-14.)

For 2000 years, Christians have been martyred, and martyred they will be during the tribulation, en masse, as the slaughter of the Christians begins. This would account for the masses of people martyred, which no man could number.

A provision has been made to protect those who are to witness for God during the holocausts. Four mighty angels, having the power to destroy the world, hold back the four winds, while an angel from the east shouted to them not to injure the earth until these servants have been sealed with the Great Seal of the Living God (Revelation 7:1-8). Note though that only Jews were sealed to be protected during the tribulation, the 144,000, 12,000 from each of the tribes of Israel.

When this persecution begins, there will be many who will turn away from Christ. There will be a falling away or rebellion against God (2 Thessalonians 2:3). There will be much sinning and hatred will abound:

"And many of you shall fall back into sin and betray and hate each other." (Matthew 24:10.)

Incomprehensible as it is, even families will turn against each other:

(12) "Brothers will betray each other to death, fathers will betray their own children, and children will betray their parents to be killed. (13) And everyone will hate you because you are mine. But all who endure to the end without renouncing me shall be saved." (Mark 13:12-13.)

It is impossible to imagine anything so horrible as families betraying each other to be killed in order to save themselves even in the face of severe persecution. But it is also difficult to imagine the indescribable tortures devised by mankind to inflict on others in order to accomplish their purposes. But the true believer in Christ endures, even unto death, the tortures, trials, and persecution, and holds firm to his faith and will be saved unto eternal life. What will enable the true Christian to endure all these things? Jesus gives this promise:

(12) ".....there will be a time of special persecution, and you will be dragged into synagogues and prisons and before kings and governors for my Name's sake. (13) But as a result, the Messiah will be widely known and honored. (14) Therefore, don't be concerned about how to answer the charges against you, (15) for I will give you the right words and such logic that none of your opponents will be able to reply!" (Luke 21:12-15.)

And Jude confirms this promise:

And he is able to keep you from slipping and falling away, and to bring you, sinless and perfect, into his glorious presence with mighty shouts of everlasting joy. Amen. (Jude 1:24.)

Therefore, the only hope of the Christian to endure is through the strength of the Holy Spirit. And those seeking to save themselves and avoid persecution, torture, or even death by worshiping the Anti-Christ and accepting his mark 666 on their arm or forehead are deluded and gain only momentary temporary relief. It does not save them. A far worse fate befalls them:

> *(9) Then a third angel followed them shouting, "Anyone worshiping the Creature from the sea and his statue and accepting his mark on the forehead or the hand, (10) must drink the wine of the anger of God; it is poured out undiluted into God's cup of wrath. (11) The smoke of their torture rises forever and ever, and they will have no relief day or night for they have worshiped the Creature and his statue and have been tattooed with the code of his name. (12) Let this encourage God's people to endure patiently every trial and persecution, for they are his saints who remain firm to the end in obedience to his commands and trust in Jesus." (Revelation 14:9-12.)*

This dreadful pronouncement of the punishment awaiting those who accept the mark 666 of the Anti-Christ on their forehead or arm should make everyone realize how important it would be to endure any persecution rather than accept that mark. They will have to endure the great wrath of God as it is poured out undiluted upon the earth during the emptying of the vials after the tribulation, and they shall have no relief day or night.

God's people, his saints, are encouraged to endure patiently every trial and persecution and even lose their earthly life rather than gain only temporary benefits. Let me reemphasize at this time that it is an elementary deduction that all this is to happen immediately prior to Christ's return; therefore, any relief gained by accepting the Anti-Christ's mark 666 would be very short lived.

The Sixth Seal: Even the sun, moon, and stars are affected:

(12) I watched as he broke the sixth seal, and there was a vast earthquake; and the sun became dark like black cloth, and the moon was blood-red. (13) Then the stars of heaven appeared to be falling to earth--like green fruit from fig trees buffeted by mighty winds. (14) And the starry heavens disappeared as though rolled up like a scroll and taken away, and every mountain and island shook and shifted.

(15) The kings of the earth, and world leaders, and rich men, and high-ranking military officers, and all men great and small, slave and free, hid themselves in the caves and rocks of the mountains and (16) cried to the mountains to crush them. "Fall on us," they pleaded, "and hide us from the face of the One sitting on the throne and from the anger of the Lamb (17) because the great day of their anger has come, and who can survive it." (Revelation 6:12-17.)

Thus fulfilling Isaiah's prophecy which says this:

For the stars of heaven and the constellations thereof shall not give their light; the sun shall be darkened in his going forth, and the moon shall not cause her light to shine. (Isaiah 13:10 KJV.)

Seventh Seal Broken: An amazing silence occurs in heaven!

(1) When the Lamb had broken the Seventh Seal, there is silence throughout all heaven for what seemed like half an hour, (2) and I saw seven angels standing before God, and they were given seven trumpets. (Revelation 8:1-2.)

Picture in your mind this magnificent spectacle as these seven mighty angels line up to blow their trumpets. The terrors of the seals are past, but the terrors of the Trumpets quickly follow.

The Trumpets:

First Trumpet: The first terror of the trumpets:

The first angel blew his trumpet, and hail, fire mixed with blood were thrown down upon earth. One-third of the earth was set on fire so that one-third of the trees were burned, and all the green grass. (Revelation 8:7.)

Second Trumpet: The second terror:

(8, 9) Then the second angel blew his trumpet, and what appeared to be a huge burning mountain was thrown into the sea, destroying a third of all the ships; and a third of the sea turned red as blood; and a third of the fish were killed. (Revelation 8:8-9.)

Third Trumpet: The third terror:

(10) The third angel blew, and a great flaming star fell from heaven upon a third of the rivers and springs. (11) The star was called Bitterness because it poisoned a third of all the water on the earth and many people died. (Revelation 8:10-11.)

Fourth Trumpet: The fourth terror. The three **Woes** are announced. Woe means extreme suffering and grief. What are these three terrible woes?

(12) The fourth angel blew his trumpet and immediately a third of the sun was blighted and darkened and a third of the moon and stars, so the daylight was dimmed by a third, and the nighttime darkness deepened. (13) As I watched, I saw a solitary eagle flying through the heavens crying loudly, "Woe, woe, woe to the people of the earth because of the terrible things that will soon happen when the three remaining angels blow their trumpets." (Revelation 8:12-13.)

Fifth Trumpet: The terror of the **first woe**. Imagine agony so great inflicted upon those who are marked with the Mark of the Beast 666 that they try to die, but death does not come and they are forced to endure this terrible punishment:

(1) Then the fifth angel blew his trumpet and I saw the one who was fallen to earth from heaven, and to him was given the key to the bottomless pit. (2) When he opened it, smoke poured out as though from some huge furnace, and the sun and air were darkened by the smoke. (3) Then locusts came from the smoke and descended onto the earth and were given power to sting like scorpions.

(4) They were told not to hurt the grass or plants or trees, but to attack those people who did not have the mark of God on their foreheads. (5) They were not to kill them, but to torture them for five months with agony like the pain of scorpion stings. (6) In those days men will try to kill themselves but won't be able to--death will not come. They will long to die--but death will flee away! (Revelation 9:1-6.)

Sixth Trumpet: The terrible **second woe**. Imagine 200 million warriors being turned loose on society, slaughtering one-third of all remaining mankind:

(13) The sixth angel blew his trumpet and I head a voice speaking from the four horns of the golden altar that stands before the throne of God, (14) saying to the sixth angel, "Release the four mighty demons held bound at the great River Euphrates." (15) They had been kept in readiness for that year and month and day and hour, and now they were turned loose to kill a third of all mankind. (16) They led an army of 200,000,000 warriors--I heard an announcement of how many there were. (Revelation 9:13-16.)

The Thunders

The Seven Thunders: Notice that there are the voices of the seven thunders between the sixth trumpet, the second woe, and the seventh trumpet, the third and most terrible of all woes. What are the Thunders saying?

> *(1) Then I saw another mighty angel coming down from heaven, surrounded by a cloud, with a rainbow over his head; his face shone like the sun and his feet flashed with fire. (2) And he held open in his hand a small scroll. He sat his right foot on the sea and his left foot on the earth, (3) and gave a great shout--it was like the roar of a lion--and the seven thunders crashed their reply. (4) I was about to write what the thunders said when a voice from heaven called to me, "Don't do it. Their words are not to be revealed."*
>
> *(5) Then the mighty angel standing on the sea and land lifted his right hand to heaven, (6) and swore by him who lives forever and ever, who created heaven and everything in it and the earth and all that it contains and the sea and its inhabitants, that there should be no more delay, (7) but that when the seventh angel blew his trumpet, then God's veiled plan--mysterious through the ages ever since it was announced by his servants the prophets--would be fulfilled. (Revelation 10:1-7.)*

It is also during this intervening period between the blowing of the sixth and seventh trumpets that we find out what happened to the two powerful witnesses referred to as olive trees and candlesticks mentioned in Zechariah 4:3, 4, 11 that God will raise up during the tribulation:

> *(3) And I will give power to my two witnesses to prophesy 1,260 days clothed in sackcloth. (4) These two prophets are the two olive trees, and two candlesticks standing before the God of all the earth. (5) Anyone trying to harm them will be killed by bursts of fire shooting from their mouths. (6) They*

have power to shut the skies so that no rain will fall during the three and a half years they prophesy, and to turn rivers and oceans to blood, and to send every kind of plague upon the earth as often as they wish. (Revelation 11:3-6.)

Who are these two witnesses? Some believe they are Elijah and Enoch, those being the only two persons, according to Scripture, who did not suffer physical death or die. Elijah was taken up in a chariot of fire (2 Kings 2:11). And Enoch just suddenly disappeared as the Lord took him (Hebrews 11:5). Some hold to the concept that these two men were spared death in preparation for their martyrdom during the tribulation:

(7) When they completed the three and a half years of their solemn testimony, the tyrant who comes out of the bottomless pit will declare war against them and conquer and kill them; and (8,9) for three and a half days their bodies will be exposed in the streets of Jerusalem (the city fittingly described as "Sodom" or "Egypt")--the very place where their Lord was crucified. No one will be allowed to bury them, and people from many nations will crowd around to gaze at them.

(10) And there will be a worldwide holiday--people everywhere will rejoice and give presents to each other and throw parties to celebrate the death of the two prophets who had tormented them so much! (11) But after three and a half days, the spirit of life from God will enter them and they will stand up! And great fear will fall on everyone.

(12) Then a loud voice will shout from heaven, "Come up!" And they will rise to heaven in a cloud as their enemies watch. (13) The same hour there will be a terrible earthquake that levels a tenth of the city, leaving 7,000 dead. Then everyone left will, in their terror, give glory to the God of heaven. The second woe is past, but the third quickly follows. (Revelation 11:7-12.)

Seventh Trumpet: And last, the terrible **third woe** of the seventh trumpet? Several things happen at the blowing of the seventh trumpet:

First, with the mighty blast of the last and seventh trumpet, there is a tremendous noise and God and his Christ takes control of the world, mankind never to rule themselves again. Picture in your mind the continued terror of remaining world populace as they begin hearing this loud voice coming from heaven telling them that the world now belongs to Christ:

> *For just then the seventh angel blew his trumpet, and there were loud voices shouting down from heaven. "The kingdom of this world now belongs to our Lord and to his Christ, and he shall reign forever and ever." (Revelation 11:15.)*

Second, at the blowing of the seventh trumpet, something tremendous is about to happen as stated by the Thunders. God's veiled plan for mankind--mysterious through the ages--is about to be fulfilled or accomplished (Revelation 10:7), indicating the Rapture or resurrection of the Christians (the church) taking place at this time.

Paul also specifically points out that the Rapture occurs at the last trumpet and gives the details of this spectacular and exciting event:

> *It will all happen in a moment, in the twinkling of an eye, when the last trumpet is blown. For there will be a trumpet blast from the sky and all Christians who have died will suddenly become alive with new bodies that will never, never die, and then we who are still alive shall suddenly have new bodies, too. (1 Corinthians 15:52.)*

The Bible does not state specifically what the terrible **third woe** of the seventh trumpet is, but I believe it would truly be a terrible woe for unbelievers when they see and recognize Christ in the clouds but they do not belong to him, and truly there could be no greater deep agonizing mourning (Matthew 24:30) all around the world, unparalleled in history, as they are left behind to watch in horror as the resurrection takes place and believers rise to meet Christ in the air (Matthew 24:31; 1 Corinthians 15:52; 1 Thessalonians 4:16) and many of their loved ones are gone. But the worst is yet to come. Unbelievers are left behind to suffer and endure the great wrath of God. Many believe that only those raptured will see Christ in the air, but Matthew 24:30 emphatically states that all nations of the world will see him arrive in the clouds at the gathering of the Christians.

That the Rapture occurs at the blowing of the seventh trumpet after the tribulation is also indicated by the fact that the 144,000 were to witness during the tribulation; yet, the 144,000, being redeemed from among men, are standing before Christ as the firstfruits unto God and **the Lamb** (Revelation 14:1-5). Firstfruits means first.

Another indication that the Rapture occurs at the blowing of the seventh trumpet is the fact that the power of God's people is not crushed (Daniel 12:7) and they are not overcome (Revelation 13:7-10) until the Anti-Christ breaks his treaty with the Jews which is three-and-a-half years after he rises to power at the beginning of the seven-year period.

Third, at the blowing of the seventh trumpet, judgment of mankind begins with servants, prophets, and saints rewarded. This further indicates that resurrection has just taken place with judgment beginning at the time of resurrection.

And the nations were angry, and thy wrath is come, and the time of the dead, that they should be judged, and that thou shouldest give reward unto thy servants the prophets, and to the saints, and them that fear thy name, small and great; and shouldest destroy them which destroy the earth. (Revelation 11:18.)

The Vials:
With the ending of the terrors of the trumpets, God's wrath is about to be poured out upon the earth. Spectacular pageantry in heaven begins as mighty angels are handed the vials containing God's wrath:

And I saw in heaven another mighty pageant showing things to come: Seven angels were assigned to carry down to earth the seven last plagues--and then at last God's anger will be finished. (Revelation 15:1.)

And one of the four Living Beings handed each of them a golden flask filled with the terrible wrath of the Living God who lives forever and forever. (Revelation 15:7.)

And I heard a mighty voice shouting from the temple to the seven angels, "Now go your ways and empty out the seven flasks of the wrath of God upon the earth." (Revelation 16:1.)

All remaining humanity who were not resurrected must endure this terrible wrath:

First Flask: *So the first angel left the temple and poured out his flask over the earth, and horrible malignant sores broke out on everyone who had the mark of the Creature and was worshiping his statute. (Revelation 16:2.)*

Second Flask: *The second angel poured out his flask upon the oceans, and they became like the watery blood of a dead man; and everything in all the oceans died. (Revelation 16:3.)*

Third Flask: *The third angel poured out his flask upon the rivers and springs and they became blood. (Revelation 16:4.)*

Fourth Flask: *(8) Then the fourth angel poured out his flask upon the sun, causing it to scorch all men with its fire. (9) Everyone was burned by this blast of heat, and they cursed the name of God who sent the plagues--they did not change their mind and attitude to give him glory. (Revelation 16:8-9.)*

Fifth Flask: *(10) Then the fifth angel poured out his flask upon the throne of the Creature from the sea and his kingdom was plunged into darkness. And his subjects gnawed their tongues in anguish, (11) and cursed the God of heaven for their pains and sores, but they refused to repent of all their evil deeds. (Revelation 16:10-11)*

Sixth Flask: *The sixth angel poured out his flask upon the great river Euphrates and it dried up so that the kings from the east could march their armies westward without hindrance. (Revelation 16:12.)*

Seventh Flask: *(17) Then the seventh angel poured out his flask into the air, and a mighty shout came from the throne of the temple of heaven, saying, "It is finished." (18) Then thunder crashed and rolled, lightening flashed, and there was a great earthquake of a magnitude unprecedented in human history.*

(19) The great city of "Babylon" split into three sections, and cities around the world fell in heaps of rubble; and so all of "Babylon's" sins were remembered in God's thoughts, and she was punished to the last drop of anger in the cup of the wine of the fierceness of his wrath.

(20) And islands vanished, and mountains flattened out, (21) and there was an incredible hailstorm from heaven; hailstones weighing a hundred pounds fall from the sky onto the people below, and they cursed God because of the terrible hail. (Revelation 16:17-21.)

With the ending of the horrors of the tribulation and pouring out of God's wrath, the terrible anger of the Living God is finally finished.

CHAPTER 7

BETWEEN DEATH AND RESURRECTION

What happens to the spirit of mankind between death and resurrection? This is a question that has been asked since time immemorial. Even the noteworthy person of Job in the Old Testament concerns himself with this same question:

> *But when a man dies and is buried, where does his spirit go? (Job 14:10.)*

Then the writer of Ecclesiastes, assumed to be the wise King Solomon, has this to say:

> *For who can prove that the spirit of man goes upward and the spirit of animals goes downward into dust. (Ecclesiastes 3:21.)*

Again, there is controversy arising out of different interpretations of Scripture concerning what happens to the spirit of man at the time of physical death and during the intermediate state between physical death and the resurrections. Some teach the human spirit of the righteous dead departs the body in a bodiless life form and ascends to be with God, while the spirit of the unrighteous dead descends into and is tormented in flames in hell *(Hades)*. Others teach soul sleep.

The teaching that the spirit ascends to God upon death is partially based on the following statement also by King Solomon:

> *Then shall the dust return to the earth as it was; and the spirit shall return unto God who gave it. (Ecclesiastes 12:7 KJV.)*

Another Scripture that is heavily relied upon is when Jesus is speaking to the thief on the cross:

Jesus said unto him, "Verily I say unto thee, today shalt thou be with me in paradise." (Luke 23:43 KJV.)

But other teachings contend that since old manuscripts had no punctuation, there is an error in punctuation; and this Scripture should read: Verily I say unto thee today, thou shalt be with me in paradise, indicating that Christ did not mean that same day but sometime in the future.

Another Scripture that is heavily relied upon that the spirit ascends to God at the time of death is from Paul's teachings:

We are confident, I say, and willing rather to be absent from the body, and to be present with the Lord. (2 Corinthians 5:8 KJV.)

Confusion arises when Scripture is taken out of context. If we read verses 1 through 7 of that same chapter 5, Paul is speaking about after the resurrection when we will be clothed with new eternal bodies:

(1) For we know that when this tent we live in now is taken down--when we die and leave these bodies--we will have wonderful new bodies in heaven, homes that will be ours forevermore, made for us by God himself, and not by human hands. (2) How weary we grow of our present bodies. That is why we look forward eagerly to the day when we shall have heavenly bodies which we shall put on like new clothes.

(3) For we shall not be merely spirits without bodies. (4) These earthly bodies make us groan and sigh, but we wouldn't like to think of dying and having no bodies at all. We want to slip into our new bodies so that these dying bodies will, as it were, be swallowed up by everlasting life. (5) This is what God has prepared for us and, as a guarantee, he has given us his Holy Spirit.

(6) Now we look forward with confidence to our heavenly bodies, realizing that every moment we spend in these earthly bodies is time spent away from our eternal home in heaven with Jesus. (7) We know these things are true by believing, not by seeing. (8) And we are not afraid but are quite content to die, for then we will be at home with the Lord. (2 Corinthians 5:1-8.)

In the above Scriptures, Paul speaks as if there were no intervening period between his own physical death and resurrection when he would receive his new body. Why? Possibly because Paul, in his early ministry, as well as other disciples, believed that Christ would come back during their lifetime. This is evidenced in the following Scriptures:

Yes, be patient. And take courage for the coming of the Lord is near. (James 5:8.)

(29) The important thing to remember is that our remaining time is very short, and so are our opportunities for doing the Lord's work. For that reason, those who have wives should stay as free as possible for the Lord, (30) happiness or sadness or wealth should not keep anyone from doing God's work. (31) Those in frequent contact with the exciting things the world offers should make good use of their opportunities without stopping to enjoy them; for the world in its present form will soon be gone. (1 Corinthians 7:29-31.)

All these things happened to them as examples--as object lessons to us--to warn us against doing the same things; they were written down so that we could read about them and learn from them in these last days as the world nears its end. (1 Corinthians 10:11.)

Some teachings relating to this intermediate state are also derived from ancient manuscripts not included in the Bible. Although these works are most fascinating to read, I do not wish to convey in any way the thought that I believe them valid.

Josephus,[28] in an extract out of his *Discourse to the Greeks Concerning Hades*, describes *Hades* as a place where the souls of the righteous and unrighteous are detained awaiting the final judgments. He calls it a place of custody for souls in which angels are appointed as guardians and give temporary punishments fitting earthly deeds. There is a lake of unquenchable fire, but no one is thrown into it until the judgments.

Josephus explains that there is but one way into this region, and an archangel stands at the gate. When the soul of man passes through this gate, he is conducted by another angel to his proper place. The righteous go to the right into a region of light. They are led there by the songs of angels who have been appointed over the place where the souls of the *just* have dwelt since the beginning of the world. They rest and wait in a state of joy for the resurrection and eternal life in heaven. And this place is called **The Bosom of Abraham.**

But the *unjust* or ungodly are dragged by force to the left by angels into a place near the lake of unquenchable fire where they hear the noise and feel the hot vapor itself. Seeing this terrible fire, they are terrified because of future judgment. Not only that, they are able to see where the righteous are but cannot cross over because there is a deep chasm between them.

Another version of this intermediate state is given in *The Book of Enoch* through visions of Enoch. Enoch XXII[29] describes *Sheol* as having four hollow places; very wide, very deep, and very smooth; three very dark and one bright. The archangel Raphael explains the purpose of the hollows as a place that all souls of the dead should assemble therein, the souls of the children of men, until judgment. One hollow is for the righteous and has a bright spring of water. And the other three hollows are for different types of sinners and the ungodly.

But it is Esdras, Greek for Ezra, in the Apocrypha,[30] that gives the most amazing account of the intermediate state between death and resurrection although he does not refer to it as *Hades* or *Sheol*. Ezra is talking to the angel who is with him:

BETWEEN DEATH AND RESURRECTION

*(75) Then I said, 'If I have won your favour, my Lord, make this plain to me: At death, when every one of us gives back his soul, shall we be kept at rest until the time when you begin to create your new world, or does our torment begin at once?'
'I will tell you that also,' he replied, 'but do not (76) include yourself among those who have despised my law; do not count yourself with those who are to be tormented. For you have a treasure of (77) good works stored up with the Most High, though you will not be shown it until the last days.*

But now to speak of death, when the Most High has given (78) final sentence for a man to die, the spirit leaves the body to return to the One who gave it, and first of all to adore the glory of the Most High. Now as for those who have rejected the ways of the Most High and despised (79) his law, and who hate all that fear God their spirits enter no settled abode, (80) but roam thenceforward in torment, grief, and sorrow. And this for seven reasons:

First, they have despised the law of the Most High. Secondly (81,82) they have lost their last chance of making a good repentance and so gaining life. Thirdly, they can see the reward in store for those who have trusted the (83) covenants of the most High. Fourthly, they begin to think of the (84) torment that awaits them at the end. Fifthly, they see the angels are (85) guarding the abode of the other souls in deep silence.

Sixthly, they see that they are (86) soon to enter into torment. The seventh cause for grief, the strongest (87) cause of all, is this: At the sight of the Most High in his glory, they break down in shame, waste away in remorse, and shrivel with fear remembering how they sinned against him in their lifetime, and how they are soon to be brought before him for judgment on the last day.

(88) As for those who have kept to the way laid down by the Most High, this is what is appointed for them when their time comes to leave their mortal (89) bodies. During their stay on earth, they served the Most High in spite of constant hardship and danger, and kept to the last letter the law given (90, 91) them by the lawgiver. Their reward is this: First, they shall exult to see the glory of God who will receive them as his own, and then they shall enter into (92) rest in seven appointed stages of joy.

Their first joy is their victory in the long fight against their inborn impulses to evil, which have failed to (93) lead them astray from life into death. Their second joy is to see the souls of the wicked wandering ceaselessly, and the punishment in store for (94) them. Their third joy is the good report given of them by their Maker, that throughout their life they kept the law with which they were entrusted.

(95) Their fourth joy is to understand the rest which they are now to share in the storehouses, guarded by angels in deep silence, and the glory waiting for (96) them in the next age. Their fifth joy is the contrast between the corruptible world they have escaped and the future life that is to be their possession, between the cramped laborious life from which they have been set free and the spacious life which will soon be theirs to enjoy for ever and ever.

(97) Their sixth joy will be the revelation that they are to shine like stars, never (98) to fade or die, with faces radiant as the sun. Their seventh joy, the greatest joy of all, will be the confident and exultant assurance which will be theirs, free from all fear and shame, as they press forward to see face to face the One whom they have served in their lifetime, and from whom they are now to receive their reward in glory. (99) The joys I have been declaring are the appointed destiny for the souls of the just; the torments I described before are the sufferings appointed for the rebellious.'

(100) Then I asked: 'When souls are separated from their bodies, will they (101) be given the opportunity to see what you have described to me?' 'They will be allowed seven days,' he replied, 'for seven days they will be permitted to see the things I have told you, and after that they will join the other souls in their abodes.' (2 Esdras 7:[75-101] The Apocrypha.)

In contrast, there are some that teach **soul sleep**; that is, death is a state of sleep and the spirit is asleep in the grave *(Sheol, Hades)* with the body during this intermediate state between physical death and resurrection. The question being that if the spirit lives on happily in the presence and glory of God, what would be the necessity of the resurrection or why would the resurrection be essential for eternal life? The hope of the Christian is the resurrection. Without the resurrection, there is no eternal life (1 Corinthians 15:13-18).

This teaching of soul sleep is objectionable to those who teach the spirit ascends to be with God at death because it deprives them of the comfort that loved ones who have died are now with God. It also deprives them of the comfort that they, too, will ascend immediately upon death to be with God. Whereas the only comfort derived from the teaching of soul sleep is the fact that whether one is in the grave thousands of years, a hundred years, or a day before the resurrection, for them it appears to be but a short time. This is evidenced by the fact that it is only while we are awake that we are aware of the passage of time. Whether we sleep for one hour or twelve hours, we are not aware while we are sleeping of how long we sleep.

Many Scriptures used to support the teaching of soul sleep because they speak of death as sleep are in 1 Thessalonians 4:13-15; John 11:11; Acts 13:36; 1 Corinthians 15:6, 18; 2 Peter 3:4; and Mark 5:39. But there are other Scriptures that imply soul sleep. When Jesus raised Lazarus from the dead, there is no mention of a continuing spiritual existence without the body. The understanding of those in that time period in direct contact with Jesus himself was that life would continue at the resurrection:

(23) Jesus told her, "Your brother shall rise again." (24) Martha saith unto him, "I know that he shall rise again in the resurrection at the last day." (John 11:23-24 KJV.)

Lazarus had been dead for four days when he was brought back to life, yet he nor any other brought back to life on earth give an account in Biblical Scripture of their soul ascending to be with God. That would have been a glorious testimony to give. It is noteworthy here to mention that to be brought back to life to die a physical death again is not the same as being resurrected never to die again.

King David also conveys the thought that his soul went into the grave along with his body:

But God will redeem my soul from the power of the grave ....." (Sheol.) (Psalms 49:15 KJV.)

For great is thy mercy toward me: and thou has delivered my soul from the lowest hell. (Sheol) (Psalms 86:13 KJV.)

And Job speaks of his total being, being hidden with the dead in *Sheol* (the grave) until after the time in future history when God's wrath has been poured out onto the world during the Great Tribulation. He asks God to remember him at the resurrection:

(11,12) As water evaporates from a Lake, as a river disappears in drought, so a man lies down for the last time and does not rise again until the heavens are no more; he shall not awaken, nor be roused from his sleep. (13) Oh, that you would hide me with the dead, and forget me there until your anger ends; but mark your calendar to think of me again! (14) If a man dies, shall he live again? This thought gives me hope, so that in all my anguish I eagerly await sweet death! (Job. 14:11-14.)

Setting aside these conflicting teachings, the most important thing to remember is that God is in control of this intermediate state also. Mankind has no control over it. And whether man's soul or spirit ascends to God upon death or sleeps until the resurrection, regardless of what is taught or believed, it will be as God dictates. We simply trust God with our soul and spirit as well as our body until that time when the resurrection takes place.

CHAPTER 8
THE RESURRECTIONS

Resurrection! Meaning that glorious event that even though we are dead, we shall come back to life again. There are two main resurrections described in the Bible, the First Resurrection (Revelation 20:5) and the last Resurrection of the dead at the Great White Throne Judgment (Revelation 20:11-13). Who will ultimately be resurrected? All humanity throughout all ages. There are two categories:

(28) Marvel not at this: for the hour is coming, in which all that are in the graves shall hear his voice, (29) And shall come forth, they that have done good, unto the resurrection of life; and they that have done evil, unto the resurrection of damnation. (John 5:28 KJV.)

And many of those whose bodies lie dead and buried will rise up, some to everlasting life and some to shame and everlasting contempt (Daniel 12:2.)

The righteous as well as the unrighteous are to be resurrected (Acts 24:15). The righteous will be resurrected to eternal life. But the unrighteous and unredeemed are raised up to shame and everlasting contempt. In this verse shame is derived from the Hebrew word *cherpah* meaning reproach. And contempt is derived from the Hebrew word *deraon* meaning a thrusting away. So these unrighteous are subjected to God's reproach and thrusting away.

The order in which the resurrections take place is not clearly defined, but the fact that the First Resurrection occurs in phases and at different times is clearly pointed out. Christ's resurrection was the first phase of this First Resurrection:

(20) But now is Christ risen from the dead, and become the firstfruits of them that slept. (22) For as in Adam all die, even so in Christ shall all be made alive. (23) But every man in his own order. Christ the firstfruits; afterward they that are in Christ's at his coming. (1 Corinthians 15:20, 22-23 KJV.)

THE RESURRECTIONS

Another phase of the First Resurrection is the 144,000 who are the firstfruits unto God and to **the Lamb:**

(1) And I looked, and, lo, a lamb stood on the mount Zion, and with him an 144,000, having his Father's name written in their foreheads. (4) These are they which were not defiled with women; for they are virgins. These are they which follow the Lamb whithersoever he goeth. These were redeemed from among men, being the firstfruits unto God and to the Lamb. (Revelation 14:1,4 KJV.)

Another phase of the First Resurrection is the two powerful witnesses who are killed after they complete their testimony at the end of the tribulation and are called up, resurrected, just prior to the blowing of the seventh trumpet:

Then a loud voice will shout from heaven, "Come up!" And they will rise to heaven in a cloud as their enemies watch (Revelation 11:12).

Yet another phase of the First Resurrection is the Rapture or resurrection of the Christians (the church), including those martyred during the Great Tribulation. This glorious event is described in the following:

(16) For the Lord himself will come down from heaven with a mighty shout and with the soul-stirring cry of the arch angel and the great trumpet call of God. And the believers who are dead will be the first to rise to meet the Lord. (17) Then we who are still alive and remain on the earth will be caught up with them in the clouds to meet the Lord in the air and remain with him forever. (1 Thessalonians. 4:16.)

And I shall send forth my angels with the sound of a mighty trumpet blast, and they shall gather my chosen ones from the farthest ends of the earth and heaven. (Matthew 24:31.)

(4) Then I saw thrones, and sitting on them were those who had been given the right to judge. And I saw the souls of those who had been beheaded for their testimony about Jesus, for proclaiming the Word of God, and who had not worshiped the Creature or his statue, nor accepted his mark on their foreheads or their hands. They had come to life again and now they reigned with Christ for a thousand years. (5) This is the First Resurrection. (The rest of the dead did not come back to life until the thousand years had ended.) (Revelation 20:4-5.)

The question is always asked: What will our resurrected bodies be like? When Christ was resurrected, although he was still in the form of man, he was changed in some manner. When he first appeared after his resurrection, even those closest to him did not recognize him until he spoke to them. Mary did not recognize him (John 20:15). Two of his followers did not recognize him (Luke 24:13-16).

Likewise, when Christ suddenly appeared to the eleven disciples, they were terrified because they thought him a spirit. The disciples were gathered behind a locked door because they were afraid of the Jewish leaders and in fear of their life after Jesus had been crucified. The door had not opened; yet suddenly Christ was standing there before them (Luke 24:36). Christ was able to simply pass through solid objects and said, ...*it is I myself. Handle me and see for a spirit has not flesh and bones, as ye see me have. (Luke 24:39 KJV.)*

And when our bodies are resurrected, they will be physically changed from a corruptible human mortal body to an immortal body that is incorruptible. We are literally born again into a new body that is not subject to the frailties of this life, imperfections, diseases, sin, and death. Paul explains why:

> *I tell you this, my brothers: An earthly body made of flesh and blood cannot get into God's kingdom. These perishable bodies of ours are not the right kind to live forever. (1 Corinthians 15:50.)*

Paul also explains the glories of the resurrected body:

(40) The angels in heaven have bodies far different from ours, and the beauty and the glory of their bodies is different from the beauty and the glory of ours. (41) The sun has one kind of glory while the moon and stars have another kind. And the stars differ from each other in their beauty and brightness. (42) In the same way, our earthly bodies which die and decay are different from the bodies we shall have when we come back to life again for they will never die.

(43) The bodies we have now embarrass us for they will become sick and die; but they will be full of glory when we come back to life again. Yes, they are weak, dying bodies now, but when we live again, they will be full of strength. (44) They are just human bodies at death; but when they come back to life, they will be superhuman bodies. For just as there are natural human bodies, there are also supernatural spiritual bodies. (1 Corinthians 15:40-44.)

Many fear death and rightly so because man fears what he cannot fully understand. Death is a fact of life, but it is also beyond man's control. God has created in us the inherent desire to live. We want to enjoy this life as long as possible.

However, as I get older, beginning my 60s in the year of 1990, death seems like the sleep we look forward to when we come home after a long hard day's work, cold, dirty, and tired, to take a nice hot bath and sink into a peaceful slumber to sleep and sleep and sleep. Storms may be raging outside; traffic going by on the streets, and trains whistling noisily as they go by, but I am oblivious to them all because I am safe, snug, and warm inside, knowing that in the morning I shall awaken refreshed and be ready for the excitement of a bright new day, or challenges (problems) of whatever life may offer.

And, to me, so it is with death after life's long weary journey; to set aside the cares and problems of the world and sink into a peaceful slumber to sleep and sleep and sleep, entrusting both soul and body to God--until I shall hear the voice of the Lord who will awaken me to a bright new day--the resurrection--for Christ said:

> *Verily, verily, I say unto you, the hour is coming, and now is, when the dead shall hear the voice of the Son of God, and they that hear shall live. (John 5:25 KJV.)*

CHAPTER 9

JUDGMENT SEAT OF CHRIST

Who will appear before Christ's Judgment Seat? Paul gives this explanation:

For we must all appear before the judgment seat of Christ, that each one may receive what is due him for the things done while in the body, whether good or bad. (2 Corinthians 5:10 NIV.)

Romans states this:

..... for we must all stand before the Judgment Seat of Christ. (Romans 14:10.)

And 1 John gives this admonishment:

And now, little children, abide in him that when he shall appear we may have confidence and not be ashamed before him at his coming. (1 John 2:28.)

When does Christ's judgment begin? As stated before, it begins at the blowing of the seventh trumpet:

(15) The seventh angel sounded his trumpet and there were loud voices in heaven which said: "The Kingdom of the world has become the kingdom of our Lord and of his Christ, and he will reign for ever and ever." (16) And the twenty-four elders, who were seated on their thrones before God, fell on their faces and worshiped God saying, (17) "We give thanks to you, Lord God Almighty, who is and who was, because you have taken your great power and have begun to reign.

(18) The nations were angry, and your wrath has come. The time has come for judging the dead, and for rewarding your

servants the prophets and your saints and those who reverence your name, both small and great--and for destroying those who destroy the earth." (Revelation 11:15-18 NIV.)

Christians, like everyone else, will be judged, punished for wrongs done in this life, and then rewarded. Christians will not be subject to the penalty of the eternal Second Death (Revelation 20:6) because Christ paid that penalty by dying on the cross; but even though the Christian is not in danger of losing eternal life, he can suffer punishment and loss of rewards. Christians have this warning:

"And that servant, which knew his Lord's will, and prepared himself not, according to his will, shall be beaten with many stripes. (48) But he that knew not, and did commit things worthy of stripes, shall be beaten with few stripes. For unto whomsoever much is given, of him shall be much required....." (Luke 12:47-48 KJV.)

The servant refers to the Christian who knew his Lord's will rather than to unbelievers. This means that Christians who do wrong knowing they are doing wrong will be punished severely, but those who do not know they are doing wrong and do wrong will not escape punishment altogether but be punished more lightly. But because Christians have been taught what is right, their responsibility is so much greater. What this punishment consists of, we are not told.

Jesus used examples that the people of his day could understand when he said, *".....beaten with many stripes,"* indicating terrible and severe punishment. The whip was used then as a means of punishment. We have all seen movies of people being flogged where the back was literally cut open with whips that had the end split into seven pieces and jagged metal pieces attached to those ends. The usual sentence was forty lashes; but because forty lashes could bring death, only thirty-nine were administered with the flogger being careful to give only thirty-nine because if he became over zealous and gave the fortieth lash, he himself was punished with a flogging.

Our stewardship of material goods are also to be judged at Christ's Judgment Seat. This admonishment is given as to earthly possessions:

(19) "Lay not up for yourselves treasures upon earth where moth and rust doth corrupt, and where thieves break through and steal; (20) but lay up for yourselves treasures in heaven where neither moth nor rust doth corrupt, and where thieves do not break through nor steal." (Matthew 6:19-20 KJV.)

How do we lay up these treasures in heaven that will survive Christ's judgment? These treasures are our works, good deeds in service to God through the utilization of what he has provided (1 Corinthians 3:12-15). The good deeds we do for others through love, for the glory of God, are counted as gold, silver, and jewels. But whatever works or good deeds we do for our own glory, self-glory, so that man will admire and praise us here on earth, that is our reward, an earthly reward of the praise we receive (Matthew 6:1-2) and will be counted as sticks, hay, and straw. The Christian's works are to be tested by fire at Christ's Judgment Seat. Works counted as gold, silver, and jewels will endure, and we will be rewarded. But if our works are counted only as sticks, hay, and straw, they will be burned, and we will suffer a great loss of rewards, even though we ourself will be saved and have eternal life, like a man escaping through a wall of flame saving nothing but himself.

Our sympathy goes out to those whose home has burned. Barely escaping themselves, they lose everything. Think how anyone would feel in that position, standing, watching everything in the world they own go up in flames. My parents had that experience when I was a little girl, and I remember how bad it was. But as bad as that is here on earth, think how anyone will feel, standing, watching eternal rewards go up in flames. We can always rebuild on earth, but there is no more time or hope for rebuilding of heavenly treasures at judgment day.

Certainly, just to have eternal life is by far more important than any other reward that can be received, so even if a person does not accept Christ as Lord until they are on their deathbed, that is far better than losing one's eternal life. But think of the tragedy of all the wasted years they could have served Christ and laid up rewards in heaven.

But it is necessary to understand that as important as service and doing good deeds are, the motive behind them is more important. The motive for doing good deeds should not be for the expectation of rewards. Why? Even if we give everything we have to the poor; and even if we were burned alive for preaching the Gospel, if we don't do those deeds out of genuine love and a desire to glorify God, these good deeds will be of no value when the testing time comes (1 Corinthians 13:3). And sadly, they will disappear like all other earthly possessions left behind when we die.

Therefore, it is important to purify our motives to determine whether service is performed for self-glory or for God's glory through love. Also, service and motives behind service determine the position Christians will hold in the new hierarchy of not only the Millennium but throughout all eternity in Christ's Kingdom. This is how to have the greater position:

(11) "The more lowly your service to others, the greater you are. To be the greatest, be a servant. (12) But those who think themselves great shall be disappointed and humbled, and those who humble themselves shall be exalted." (Matthew 23:11-12.)

Service to God begins with reverence and worship. God expects us to worship him. Service ends with what we do to help others. We can all ask these questions: What have I done with the life God gave me? Does my life glorify God? What will Christ see when I stand before him in judgment?

After the Judgment Seat of Christ is completed, the Wedding Banquet of Christ is about to take place. Who will be invited to this great celebration? The true Christians, the church, the bride:

(7) Let us be glad and rejoice and honor him; for the time has come for the wedding banquet of the Lamb, and his bride has prepared herself. (8) She is permitted to wear the cleanest and whitest and finest of linens. (Fine linen represent the good deeds done by the people of God). (9) And the angel dictated this sentence to me: "Blessed are those who are invited to the wedding feast of the Lamb." And he added, "God himself has stated this." (Revelation 19:7-9.)

How fortunate Christians are that in making Christ their Lord and Saviour they have the opportunity to be invited to this magnificent wedding banquet of Christ, just prior to the Second Coming of Christ to begin his Millennium reign.

CHAPTER 10

THE SECOND COMING OF CHRIST

The time for the long-awaited Second Coming of Christ to set up his earthly kingdom and begin his Millennium reign appears to be approaching at an accelerated pace. At the time of Christ's birth, the Jews looked for a Messiah or leader who would restore Israel to greatness. Even today, followers of Christ want him to exercise his great power in righting the wrongs of the world. But this will only happen at his Second Coming when he establishes a monarchy to control and rule the whole world. Then he will come with power, great power. What a glorious sight that will be! This tremendous event is described below:

> *(11) Then I saw heaven opened and a white horse standing there; and the one sitting on the horse was named "Faithful and True"--the one who justly punishes and makes war. (12) His eyes were like flames, and on his head were many crowns. A name was written on his forehead, and only he knew its meaning. (13) He was clothed with garments dipped in blood and his title was "The Word of God." (14) The armies of heaven, dressed in finest linen, white and clean, followed him on white horses. (15) In his mouth he held a sharp sword to strike down the nations; he ruled them with an iron grip; and he trod the winepress of the fierceness of the wrath of Almighty God. (Revelation 19:11-15.)*

The magnificent white horse perhaps represents the purity of Christ and the peace he brings to the Millennium. His name is Faithful and True designating trustworthiness and truth. There is no doubt that the one sitting thereon is Christ himself, his power absolute represented by the sharp sword in his mouth. Whatever punishment he metes out to the surviving world population will be fair and just as he crushes the power of all nations through war with all the fury of the wrath of Almighty God in his takeover of the world.

His eyes are flaming like fire representing penetrating insight, and his many crowns represent his rulership over all nations of the world. Only he knows the meaning of the name written on his forehead. His clothes are dipped in blood which could be a symbolism of the sacrificial shedding of his own blood for mankind or the blood shed by his followers who were martyred.

In addition to the name written on his forehead, he has another title which is "The Word of God." We learned from John 1:1-3 that Christ is Creator of all things in heaven and on earth and carries out God's spoken word; therefore, he has the title of The Word of God. These armies of heaven following Christ represent Christ's bride, resurrected Christians, the church. The fine linen represents their good deeds (Revelation 19:8), and white and clean represents purity from having been cleansed by the blood of Christ (Revelation 7:14).

Then an angel is calling the birds to prepare to consume and cleanse the earth of the dead as the Evil Creature (Anti-Christ) gathers the armies of the governments to fight a hopeless battle (Revelation 16:16) in the great **Battle of Armageddon**:

> *(17) Then I saw an angel standing in the sunshine, shouting loudly to the birds, 'Come! Gather together for the supper of the Great God! (18) Come and eat the flesh of kings, and captains, and great generals; of horses and riders; and of all humanity, both great and small, slave and free. (19) Then I saw the Evil Creature gathering the governments of the earth and their armies to fight against the one sitting on the horse and his army.*

> *(20) And the Evil Creature was captured, and with him the False Prophet, who could do mighty miracles when the Evil Creature was present--miracles that deceived all who had accepted the Evil Creature's mark, and who worshiped his statue. Both of them--the Evil Creature and his False Prophet--were thrown alive into the Lake of Fire that burns with sulphur. (21) And their entire army was killed with the sharp sword in the mouth of the one riding the white horse, and all the birds of heaven were gorged with their flesh. (Revelation 19:17-21.)*

Christ kills both animals and riders alike, the entire army by supernatural powers, represented by the sword in his mouth. The Anti-Christ and False Prophet are captured and **thrown alive** into the Lake of Fire. What a horrible fate! Thus, this Age will draw to a close and the New Age will begin in which there will truly be *a new world order*, The Millennium.

CHAPTER 11
THE MILLENNIUM

The long-awaited utopia that man has yearned for, looked for, and hoped for will arrive in its proper time. This Age, the Age of Grace, or this dispensation will pass away, and the New Age, the Millennium will begin.

Today, we live in a world where **might** makes **right**! So will it be during the Millennium. Many believe the Millennium will be the utopia of all time because everyone will willingly follow Christ, but it will be a utopia only because Christ will rule with a rod of iron, an unyielding grip as strong as iron. He will strike down those who do not obey his laws. There can be no doubt as to his Lordship. On his robe and thighs are written another title, King of Kings and Lord of Lords (Revelation 19:15).

With the coming of the Millennium, yet another terrible judgment is to befall mankind, the **judgment of the living,** those left alive on earth after all the holocausts of the tribulation and the pouring out of the wrath of God.

Most of world population has been killed. Thousands upon thousands of people have died during the holocausts of the tribulation. Specifically one-fourth of all mankind was killed with war, famine, disease, and wild animals at the breaking of the Fourth Seal (Revelation 6:8). Many people of the remaining population died at the blowing of the Third Trumpet when one-third of all the earth's water is poisoned (Revelation 8:11). At the blowing of the Sixth Trumpet, one-third of what was left of mankind was killed by the 200,000,000 soldiers (Revelation 9:15). And all the armies of the governments of the earth were killed at the Battle of Armageddon (Revelation 16:16, 19:21). Millions of Christians during the tribulation were martyred (Revelation 6:9-11; 7:9-14).

The Judgment of the Living of remaining world populace will determine who is to enter into this golden Millennium Age. What a magnificent sight that will be with Christ surrounded by millions of angels. Christ will then sit on his throne in all his splendor and glory:

(31) But when I, the Messiah, shall come in my glory, and all the angels with me, then I shall sit upon my throne of glory. And all the nations shall be gathered before me. (32) And I will separate the people as a shepherd separates the sheep from the goats (33) and place the sheep at my right hand and the goats at my left.

(34) Then I, the King, shall say to those at my right, "Come, blessed of my Father, into the Kingdom prepared for you from the founding of the world. (35) For I was hungry and you fed me; I was thirsty and you gave me water; I was a stranger and you invited me into your homes; (36) naked and you clothed me; sick and in prison, and you visited me."

(37) Then these righteous ones will reply, "Lord, when did we ever see you hungry and feed you? Or thirsty and give you anything to drink? (38) Or a stranger, and help you? Or naked, and clothe you? (39) When did we ever see you sick or in prison, and visit you?" (40) And I, the King, will tell them, "When you did it to these my brothers you were doing it to me!" (Matthew 25:31-36.)

The criteria for being among those to enter the Millennium, the sheep, in this prophecy appears to be in their treatment of the Jews, his brothers, during the severe persecution and perilous time for Israel during the tribulation, many at the peril of their own life. This is evidenced by their care of the hungry, thirsty, naked, sick, homeless, and imprisoned.

Indeed, these seem surprised that they are the blessed who are to enter into the Millennium. They asked Christ when it was that they had they seen him hungry, thirsty, naked, sick, homeless, or imprisoned. He tells them that their treatment of his brothers was the same as if it were to himself in person. Those who would not accept the Anti-Christ's mark 666 on their forehead or arm could not buy, sell, or work to provide for themselves (Revelation 13:17), thus they needed help! Those counted righteous then pass into the Millennium.

But a terrible judgment is then pronounced on those on the left, the goats. They are sent away to be thrown into the Lake of Fire.

(41) Then I will turn to those on my left and say, "Away with you, you cursed ones, into the eternal fire prepared for the devil and his demons. (42) For I was hungry and you wouldn't feed me; thirsty and you wouldn't give me anything to drink; (43) a stranger, and you refused me hospitality, naked, and you wouldn't clothe me, sick and in prison, and you didn't visit me."

(44) Then they will reply, "Lord, when did we ever see you hungry or thirsty or a stranger or naked or sick or in prison, and not help you?" (45) And I will answer, "When you refused to help the least of these my brothers, you were refusing help to me." (46) And they shall go away into eternal punishment, but the righteous into everlasting life. (Matthew 25:41-46.)

What will life be like during the Millennium? Much is said about the Millennium but little is known about what daily life will actually be like during this era. As those counted righteous enter en masse into the New Age or Millennium, these are mortal human beings. Just as in the days of Noah after the Great Flood when the earth was repopulated by Noah's family, the world is to be repopulated by Israel during the Millennium with a thousand years of generations. Israel will blossom and fill the earth (Isaiah 27:6) fulfilling promises to Abraham that his seed would be as the sands of the seas (Genesis 17:2-8).

Imagine the condition the world will be in after the holocausts. But just as there has been a rebuilding and restoring after each successive war throughout history and the Twentieth Century, so will there be a rebuilding and restoring after the devastation of the tribulation.

Through a study of the Millennium, there is just a glimmer of the hierarchy that Christ will establish during his thousand-year reign. Those who have been given the right to judge are on their thrones ready to begin their reign with him, including all those martyred and beheaded during the tribulation (Revelation 20:4). These are now immortal beings that will be a part of the ruling government on this same earth we live in today ruling over mortal human beings where life as usual continues with marriages and families that repopulate the earth.

And all nations, having been totally shattered by Christ's power upon his coming to set up his long-prophesied Kingdom will be remolded according to God's will as Christ gives those reigning with him the power to rule with a rod of iron just as the Father has given him this power:

> *(26) To every one who overcomes--who to the very end keeps on doing things that please me--I will give power over the nations. (27) You will rule them with a rod of iron just as my Father gave me the authority to rule them; they will be shattered like a pot of clay that is broken into tiny pieces. (Revelation 2:26-27.)*

Scripture does not specify what special joys, above mortal joys, God has in store for Christians during that time since there are no marriage relationships among the immortal (Luke 20:34-36; Mark 12:24-25; Matthew 22:29-30). But if the Christian of today can ever grasp the magnitude of the position he is to have in the hierarchy of God's order as co-rulers during the Millennium, he can perhaps just begin to appreciate the value of the priceless gift of eternal life.

The following are just a few of the many Scriptures given by Old Testament prophets pertaining to the prophecies of the Millennium and the ultimate destiny of Israel. First, there will be a time of great mourning:

> *(8) The Lord will defend the people of Jerusalem; the weakest among them will be as mighty as King David! And the royal line will be as God, like the Angel of the Lord who goes before them! (9) For my plan is to destroy all nations that come against Jerusalem. (10) Then I will pour out the*

> *spirit of grace and prayer on all the people of Jerusalem, and they will look on him they pierced, and mourn for him as for an only son, and grieve bitterly for him as for an oldest child who dies.*
>
> *(11) The sorrow and mourning in Jerusalem at that time will be even greater than the grievous mourning for the godly King Josiah, who was killed in the Valley of Megiddo. (12,13,14) All of Israel will be in profound sorrow. The whole nation will be bowed down with universal grief--king, prophet, priest, and people. Each family will go into private mourning, husbands and wives apart, to face their sorrow alone. (Zechariah 12:8-14.)*

When the Egyptians went to the aid of the Assyrians in their last stand against the onslaught of the great Babylonian army, Israel's beloved King Josiah, who had brought about more reforms than any other king, was killed in battle at Megiddo (2 Kings 23:29).

Israel will never again worship idols nor stray away from God, and any enemies of Israel (the thorns and briars, meaning other nations) will be destroyed unless they adhere to God's ruling.

> *(3) Israel is my vineyard; I, the Lord, will tend the fruitful vines. Everyday I'll water them, and day and night I'll watch to keep all enemies away. (4,5) My anger against Israel is gone. If I find thorns and briars bothering her, I will burn them up, unless these enemies of mine surrender and beg for peace and my protection. (6) The time will come when Israel will take root and bud and blossom and fill the whole earth with her fruit!*
>
> *(7,8) Has God punished Israel as much as he has punished her enemies? No, for he has devastated her enemies, while he has punished Israel but a little, exiling her far from her own land as though blown away in a storm from the east. (9) And why did God do it? It was to purge away her sins, to rid*

her of all her idol altars and her idols. They will never be worshiped again. (Isaiah 27:3-9.)

Many confuse the Millennium with eternity thinking there will be no pain, tears, or death; but **there will be some death.** Israel will be purified. Everyone will worship the Lord. Parents will even kill their own children who do not honor the Lord:

(1) At that time a Fountain will be opened to the people of Israel and Jerusalem, a Fountain to cleanse them from all their sins and uncleanness. (2) And the Lord of Hosts declares, "In that day I will get rid of every vestige of idol worship throughout the land, so that even the names of the idols will be forgotten. All false prophets and fortune-tellers will be wiped out, (3) and if anyone begins false prophecy again, his own father and mother will slay him! 'You must die,' they will tell him, 'for you are prophesying lies in the name of the Lord.'" (Zechariah 13:1-3.)

But Isaiah proclaims there will also come a time of great joy for Israel:

(18) Look, I will recreate Jerusalem as a place of happiness, her people shall be a joy! (19) And I will rejoice in Jerusalem, and in my people; and the voice of weeping and crying shall not be heard there any more. (20) No longer will babies die when only a few days old; no longer will men be considered old at 100! Only sinners will die that young.

(21,22) In those days, when a man builds a house, he will keep on living in it--it will not be destroyed by invading armies as in the past. My people will plant vineyards and eat the fruit themselves. Their enemies will not confiscate it. For my people will live as long as trees and will long enjoy their hard-won gains. (23) Their harvest will not be eaten by their enemies; their children will not be born to be cannon fodder.

THE MILLENNIUM

For they are the children of those the Lord has blessed; and their children, too, shall be blessed.

(24) I will answer them before they even call to me. While they are still talking to me about their needs, I will go ahead and answer their prayers! (25) The wolf and Lamb shall feed together, the lion shall eat straw as the ox does, and poisonous snakes shall strike no more! In those days nothing and no one shall be hurt or destroyed in all my Holy Mountain says the Lord. (Isaiah 65:18-25.)

There will be no more wars:

(2) In the last days, Jerusalem and the Temple of the Lord will become the world's greatest attraction, and people from many lands will flow there to worship the Lord. (3) "Come," everyone will say, "Let us go up the mountain of the Lord, to the Temple of the God of Israel; there he will teach us his laws, and we will obey them." For in those days the world will be ruled from Jerusalem. (4) The Lord will settle international disputes; all the nations will convert their weapons of war into implements of peace. Then at last all wars will stop and all military training will end. (Isaiah 2:2-4.)

Crime will no longer be rampant. There will be no Supreme Court, no appeals, as in our justice system today which has deteriorated to the point that it is no longer a question of guilt of the criminal and punishment for the crime; it is whether or not criminals' rights have been protected; therefore, criminal after criminal is turned loose back on society to murder, rape, and rob, because of legal technicalities. But it will not be so in that day; the lawless and ungodly will die (Isaiah 65:20). The manner of execution is not stated.

Peace and justice and equality will finally abound, and the inequities of life will disappear during Christ's reign here on earth:

His ever-expanding, peaceful government will never end. He will rule with perfect fairness and justice from the throne of his father David. He will bring true justice and peace to all the nations of the world. (Isaiah 9:7.)

And there will be only one world-wide ruler and only the true God shall be worshiped throughout the whole earth thus fulfilling the prophecies of thousands of years ago of promises to King David that his descendants would rule forever (2 Samuel 7:8-16), as Christ's reign extends into eternity (Revelation 21:22):

And the Lord shall be King over all the earth. In that day there will be one Lord. His name alone will be worshiped. (Zechariah 14:9.)

At the end of the Millennium, Satan will be let out again to deceive the nations. How many are deceived? A mighty host, numberless as the sand along the seashore:

(7) When the thousand years end, Satan will be let out of his prison. (8) He will go out to deceive the nations of the world and gather them together, with Gog and Magog, for battle--a mighty host, numberless as sand along the shore. (9) They will go up across the broad plain of the earth and surround God's people and the beloved city of Jerusalem on every side. But fire from God in heaven will flash down on the attacking armies and consume them. (10) Then the Devil who had betrayed them will be thrown into the Lake of Fire burning with sulphur where the Creature and False Prophet are, and they will be tormented day and night forever and ever. (Revelation 20:7-10.)

It is incomprehensible that after living under the rule of perfect justice and peace for 1000 years that there would be those who would rebel against Christ, especially knowing this prophecy that they will be destroyed by fire from God. But as generation after generation is born during the Millennium and multitudes of people fill the earth, it will be just as in the days of Noah. Noah was counted a righteous man; but numberless masses of subsequent generations did not retain that righteousness. So it will be at the end of the Millennium when Satan is turned loose on the world again. There will always be those who rebel against authority and law and order and disregard the laws of God if they are given the choice.

With the ending of the Millennium, Satan is judged and punished by being thrown into the Lake of Fire (Revelation 20:10); and the final judgment of mankind, judgment of the dead, takes place in the Great White Throne Judgment.

CHAPTER 12

GREAT WHITE THRONE JUDGMENT

This is the prophecy of the last Resurrection and final disposition of mankind at the **Judgment of the Dead** by God Almighty himself, after the Millennium, before the Second Death and beginning of eternity. Daniel gives a detailed description of this Great White Throne Judgment:

> *I watched as thrones were put in place and the Ancient of Days--the Almighty God--sat down to judge. His clothing was as white as snow, his hair like whitest wool. He sat upon a fiery throne brought in on flaming wheels, and a river of fire flowed from before him. Millions of angels ministered to him; and hundreds of millions of people stood before him, waiting to be judged. Then the court began its session and The Books were opened. (Daniel 7:9-10.)*

And a further description of this dreadful judgment that is to fall upon mankind is given:

> *And I saw a great white throne and the one who sat upon it, from whose face the earth and sky fled away, but they found no place to hide. I saw the dead, great and small, standing before God; and The Books were opened, including the Book of Life. And the dead were judged according to the things written in The Books, each according to the deeds he had done. The oceans surrendered the bodies buried in them; and the earth and the underworld gave up the dead in them. Each was judged according to his deeds. (Revelation 20:11-12.)*

Who then are these dead who have been resurrected to be judged by God Almighty himself? All humanity who have died throughout all Ages, except those who have already been resurrected in the First Resurrection. Why did the earth and sky flee from the face of God, and why was there no place for the dead to stand before God at this resurrection and judgment? Peter answers this question:

GREAT WHITE THRONE JUDGMENT

..... the heavens will pass away with a terrible noise and the heavenly bodies will disappear in fire, and the earth and everything on it will be burned up. (2 Peter 3:10.)

Why were The Books opened? God is a just God, and each is judged according to his own deeds, indicating degrees of punishment. No one will suffer punishment for someone else's wrongful acts. The Book of Life is also opened. Scripture does not identify who among these dead standing before God would be recorded in the Book of Life. Every person's name has been entered into the Book of Life, but the names of the ungodly has been blotted out (Revelation 3:5). The Book of Life is searched to see if anyone's name is found. If their name is not found, they are thrown into the Lake of Fire along with Death and Hell (*Sheol and Hades*):

And Death and Hell were thrown into the Lake of Fire. This is the Second Death--the Lake of Fire. And if anyone's name was not found recorded in the Book of Life, he was thrown into the Lake of Fire. (Revelation 20:14-15.)

There will be no more death, no more graves after the Second Death. How wonderful that will be! Only those who have stood at the side of the grave of a loved one on a cold, wet, wintery day can truly appreciate the significance of what this means. I shall never forget the look of anguish more than forty years ago on my sister Mozelle's face as we stood at the grave side of her only daughter, ten years old. My high heels buried in the mud, I could not even get to her before she turned and walked away. She did not even see me as I stood helplessly reaching out to her with my hand. A few years later, we buried our father and mother, then a brother, since then other brothers and sisters.

Fortunate indeed are the Christians not included in this terrible judgment because having been included in the First Resurrection, this judgment and the Second Death has no power over them (Revelation 20:6). And how fortunate Christians are and how thankful they should be to be judged by Christ instead of Almighty God. Why? *It*

is a fearful thing to fall into the hands of the Living God. (Hebrews 10:31 KJV.)
   At the conclusion of the Great White Throne Judgment, all unredeemed humanity of all Ages are sentenced to the dreadful and everlasting punishment of the Second Death.

CHAPTER 13

THE SECOND DEATH AND HELL

What is the Second Death? What is Hell? It is a final and everlasting punishment for mankind and fallen angels from which there is no resurrection. Paul gives the description of those consigned to this dreadful punishment:

> *Who shall be punished with everlasting destruction from the presence of the Lord and from the glory of his power. (2 Thessalonians 1:9 KJV.)*

The root word for destruction in the above verse is the Greek word *Olethros* which means destruction. And the destruction of Death, Hades, and mankind are described below:

> *(14) And Death and Hades were thrown into the Lake of Fire. This is the Second Death--the Lake of Fire. (15) And if anyone's name was not found recorded in the Book of Life, he was thrown into the Lake of Fire. (Revelation 20:14-15.)*

What then is hell? Hell then is the everlasting Second Death. But there are also controversial teachings pertaining to the actual meaning of hell as related to the Second Death. There are basically two interpretations of Scriptures relating to hell:

Some teach this punishment of the Second Death means immortality of the resurrected body and soul, separated from God, burning in flames in eternal torment, a continuing existence in a state of punishment that lasts forever for unredeemed mankind and fallen angels in the Lake of Fire.

Some teach destruction of both body and soul with a total absence of life in eternal death where that person would cease to exist, just as if they had never been born. A punishment that is everlasting for unredeemed mankind and fallen angels in the Lake of Fire, as God's way of disposing of useless refuse.

Unfortunately, there are Scriptures that presumably support both interpretations. Some Scriptures appear to support the interpretation of **eternal torment** while there are some that point toward **eternal death**. Both interpretations acknowledge that this punishment is everlasting, forever (Matthew 25:46).

In considering these two concepts of eternal punishment, there is a vast difference between being in a state of punishment that lasts forever and everlasting punishment. For example, the condemned criminal sentenced to life without parole in prison, he continues to exist in a state of punishment for as long as he lives. Whereas, the condemned criminal sentenced to death and executed cannot be brought back to life so his punishment is everlasting, forever, as far as his earthly life is concerned; but he will not continue to experience the physical act of dying or the torment and agony of knowing that he is going to be put to death, and the physical pain he suffers during the execution itself does not last forever.

In order to grasp the meaning of hell as interpreted in the Bible, it is necessary to understand that the word hell is translated from four root words:

1. The Hebrew word *Sheol* in the Old Testament.
2. The Greek word *Hades* in the New Testament.
3. The Greek word *Tartaroo* in the New Testament.
4. The Greek word *Gehenna* in the New Testament.

Confusion arises when Christian theologians, preachers, and evangelists preach hell inclusive as the place where the soul of unredeemed mankind goes at the time of physical death to burn in fire and torment from then on for all eternity. Being almost universally taught this concept, we automatically bring to mind the Second Death when we hear the word hell. But if you look up the root word and its definition in Young's Analytical Concordance to the Bible,[31] you will find this:

Sheol (Hebrew of the Old Testament) and *Hades* (Greek of the New Testament) in the Bible, both meaning the unseen state or world, literally the grave or intermediate state between physical death and resurrection are translated as follows in the Bible:

Sheol is translated *hell* in Deuteronomy 32:22; 2 Samuel 22:6; Job 11:8, 26:6; Psalms 9:17, 16:10, 18:5, 55:15, 86:13, 116:3, 139:8; Proverbs 5:5, 7:27, 9:18, 15:11, 15:24, 23:14, 27:20; Isaiah

THE SECOND DEATH AND HELL

5:14, 14:9, 14:15, 28:15, 28:18, 57:9; Ezekiel 31:16, 31:17, 32:21, 32:27; Amos 9:2; Jonah 2:2; and Habakkuk 2:5.

Sheol is translated *grave* in Genesis 37:35, 42:38, 44:29, 44:31; 1 Samuel 2:6; 1 Kings 2:6, 2:9; Job 7:9, 14:13, 17:13, 21:13, 24:19; Psalms 6:5, 30:3, 31:17, 49:14, 49:15, 88:3, 89:48, 141:7; Proverbs 1:12, 30:16; Ecclesiastes 9:10; Song of Solomon 8:6; Isaiah 14:11, 38:10, 38:18; Ezekiel 31:15; and Hosea 13:14.

Sheol is translated *pit* in Numbers 16:30, 16:33; Job 17:16.

Hades is translated *hell* in Matthew 11:23, 16:18; Luke 10:15, 16:23; Acts 2:27, 2:31; and Revelation 1:18, 6:8, 20:13, 20:14.

Hades is translated *grave* in 1 Corinthians 15:55.

Tartaroo translated *hell* meaning abyss or prison is referred to only one time in the Bible and does not pertain to man at all but to fallen angels. Here they await final judgment. It is amazing that while man suffers physical death while awaiting final judgment, fallen angels are not subject to physical death but are condemned to live in darkness while awaiting judgment. How terrible to be confined in darkness all those thousands of years never seeing light. The root word for hell in the verse below is *Tartaroo*:

> *For God did not spare even the angels who sinned, but threw them into hell, chained in gloomy caves and darkness until the judgment day. (2 Peter 2:4.)*

Gehenna translated *hell* (fire) is used only twelve times in the Bible. It is found in Matthew 5:22, 5:29, 10:28, 18:9, 23:15, 23:33; Mark 9:43, 9:45, 9:47; Luke 12:5; James 3:6; and 2 Peter 2:4.

It refers to the Valley of Hinnom, which was Jerusalem's continuously burning garbage dump where all manner of refuse was thrown, including the bodies of dead animals, criminals, and beggars who had no means of proper burial. The fire never went out; and bodies left on the outer fringes of the fire didn't burn and became infested with maggots. Therefore, the worm never died out either (Isaiah 66:24: Mark 9:44).

This *Gehenna* hell (fire) is used to illustrate and convey the message of final punishment and the finality of the everlasting Second

Death in the Lake of Fire. It is this Lake of Fire at the Second Death that death and hell *(Sheol and Hades)* are to be cast into (Revelation 20:14) meaning there will be no more death and no need for graves or the unseen state, so both are destroyed in the Second Death and cease to exist.

The word "Torment" is used in the Bible only twenty-one times, and this is in the New Testament. The four Greek words for torment are:

(1) *Basanismos*, meaning a trial, testing, torment.
(2) *Basanos*, meaning a test, trial, inquisition, torment.
(3) *Basanizo,* to try, test, torment.
(4) *Odunaomai*, meaning to be pained.

Part of the basis for the concept of eternal torment is found primarily in six Scriptures; and of those six, only two are found in Revelation. The other four are found in the parable of the rich man in *Hades* and a beggar named Lazarus in Luke 16:19-31 in which the rich man talked about being tormented in flames. However, *Hades* is the grave and intermediate state between physical death and the resurrections. The usage of flames used to illustrate the Lake of Fire in the Second Death refers only to *Gehenna*.

Jesus used parables (stories) many times to illustrate a point. He translated many of his parables to clarify their true meaning. Unfortunately, he did not translate this difficult to understand parable of the rich man and Lazarus. Some dogmatically teach that the rich man and beggar represent two individual personages and the scene depicted is literal and clearly substantiates the concept of eternal torment. However, as pointed out previously, *Hades* is not a place of flames.

A religion called the Divine Plan[32] in an article *What Say the Scriptures About Hell* which I received unsolicited in the mail in the 1960s, with much modesty also offer this different and realistic interpretation of this particular parable: That since Jesus used terms such as seeds, wheat, thistles, sheep, goats, kings and servants to represent classes of people in many of his parables, the rich man and beggar also represent classes of people which are presented as follows:

THE SECOND DEATH AND HELL

Abraham in the parable represents God, and the rich man clothed in purple and fine linen represent the Jews. The Jews fared as royalty with the riches of divine favor, care, and protection as God's chosen while the beggar names Lazarus, representing the Gentiles, remained outside this circle. The name Lazarus means with no help or helped of God. The pitiful condition of the beggar describes exactly the magnitude of the state the Gentiles were in, dead in their sins, lost without hope, in desperate need of God's help.

Each, the Jews and Gentiles, died to their present state, the end of that age having come. The Jews (represented by the rich man), having rejected their Messiah Christ, was cut off and will remain cut off until the time for the Gentile has ended. And the anguish of their cries has been heard throughout the centuries; the chasm between salvation through faith (belief in Christ) and salvation by adhering to the law being too wide and too deep to cross. But the Gentiles (represented by the beggar Lazarus), accepting Christ as their Saviour, find themselves adopted into the family of Abraham, safe in the arms of God.

Who is Abraham? Abraham lived in the 9th generation (Genesis 11:26) from Shem who was a son of Noah. Known as father of multitudes, he was the progenitor of the Hebrew race which later became known as the Jews.

The first specific reference in Revelation used to support the concept of eternal torment in relation to the Second Death probably relates to the torment of those during the wrath of God being poured out undiluted upon the earth in which they have no relief night or day:

> *(9) Then a third angel followed them shouting, "Anyone worshiping the Creature from the sea and his statue (10) must drink the wine of the anger of God; it is poured out undiluted into God's cup of wrath. And they will be tormented with fire and burning sulphur in the presence of the holy angels and the Lamb. (11) The smoke of their torture rises forever and ever, and they will have no relief day or night, for they have worshiped the Creature and his statue, and have been tattooed with the code of his name." (Revelation 14:9-11.)*

Some interpret this Scripture to refer to the state of unredeemed mankind throughout all eternity; however, this Scripture clearly points out that it is those who worshiped the Creature (Anti-Christ) and his statue who will be tormented with fire as God's wrath is poured out on mankind.

Notice that it is the smoke that rises forever and ever. In Isaiah 34:10 and Revelation 19:3, smoke rising forever and ever is symbolic of the finality of destruction; while in Isaiah 6:4 and Revelation 15:8, smoke filling the Temple represents the great power and glory of God which we know is forever and ever. This torment of fire inflicted upon mankind with no relief day or night during God's wrath is described as follows:

(8) Then the fourth angel poured out his flask upon the sun, causing it to scorch all men with its fire. (9) Everyone was burned by this blast of heat.....(10) The fifth angel poured out his flask upon the throne of the Creature from the sea, and his kingdom was plunged into darkness. And his subjects gnawed their tongues in anguish. (Revelation 16:8-10.)

The second specific and possibly strongest reference in Revelation used to support the concept of eternal torment is Revelation 20:10 when Satan, the Devil, is thrown into the Lake of Fire. The Greek word for tormented used in this verse is *basanizo* meaning to try, test, torment:

Then the Devil who had betrayed them will again be thrown into the Lake of Fire burning with sulphur where the Creature and False Prophet are, and they will be tormented day and night forever and ever. (Revelation 20:10.)

Over the many years, I have also read books by noted authors and heard sermons during revivals and services in different churches pertaining to the concept of eternal torment that referred to ancient writings not included in the Bible. New Testament writers were also well acquainted with Old Testament and ancient writings. Mark 9:48

possibly refers to Jerusalem's continuous burning garbage dump used to illustrate the Second Death or to the work of Josephus.

Josephus,[33] the renowned Jewish historian, describes his concept of eternal torment for man: That every body shall have its own soul restored to it at the resurrection; that the righteous will receive a changed, whole, well, pure body; but the unrighteous will receive the same body with the same deformities and diseases they died with. The righteous will have the just reward of eternal life, while the unrighteous will go into the unquenchable fire and be tormented as follows:

> "..... and a certain fiery worm never dying, and not destroying the body, but continuing its eruption out of the body with never-ceasing grief, neither will sleep give ease to these men, nor will the night afford them comfort; death will not free them from their punishment ....."

The *Book of Enoch* describes Enoch's vision of eternal torment for the angels:

> *(7) And from thence I went to another place, which was still more horrible than the former, and I saw a horrible thing: A great fire there which burnt and blazed, and the places was cleft as far as the abyss, being full of great descending columns of fire; neither its extent or magnitude could I see, nor could I conjecture. (8) Then I said, 'How fearful is the place and how terrible to look upon!' (9) Then Uriel answered me, one of the holy angels who was with me, and said unto me, 'Enoch, why has thou such fear and affright?' And I answered, 'Because of this fearful place, and because of the spectacle of the pain.' (10) And he said unto me, 'This place is the prison of the angels, and here they will be imprisoned for ever.' (XXI, 7-10, Book of Enoch.)*

Pertaining to the concept of **eternal death**, there many Scriptures that specifically and emphatically state over and over that Satan and his demons, the Anti-Christ, the False Prophet, and unredeemed mankind will go to destruction, perish, be destroyed in the Lake of Fire at the Second Death, death being the absence of life, and this punishment of destruction is to be forever, everlasting.

It is Ezekiel who explains about this final destruction of Satan (Lucifer); that he shall be no more:

> *(18) You defiled your holiness with lust for gain, therefore I brought forth fire from your own actions and let it burn you to ashes upon the earth in sight of all those watching you. (19) All who know you are appalled at your fate; you are an example of horror; you are destroyed forever. (Ezekiel 28:18-19.)*

Then the following Scriptures point to eternal death by the usage of the Greek word *apoleia* meaning loss, destruction.

Christ himself speaks of the destruction of Satan (Lucifer). The root word for destruction in the following verse is *apoleia*:

> *"While I was with them, I protected them and kept them safe by that name you gave me. None has been lost except the one doomed to destruction so that Scripture would be fulfilled." (John 17:12 NIV.)*

Then in the destruction of the Anti-Christ, who is Satan's pawn during the period of the Great Tribulation, when he comes out of the bottomless pit--bottomless pit being translated from the Greek word *abussos* meaning a very deep place--the root word for destruction is *apoleia*:

> *..... And yet, soon he will come up out of the bottomless pit and go to eternal destruction .....(Revelation 17:8.)*

As explained before about the Anti-Christ being the eighth king, the root word for doom below is *apoleia*:

> *The scarlet animal that died is the eighth king, having reigned before as one of the seven; after his second reign he too will go to his doom. (Revelation 17:11.)*

Paul also speaks of the Anti-Christ's destruction. The root word for destruction is *apoleia*:

> *Don't let anyone deceive you in any way, for that day will not come until rebellion occurs and the man of lawlessness is revealed, the man doomed to destruction. (2 Thessalonians 2:3 NIV.)*

And it is Paul who describes mankind's destruction. Again, the root word for destroyed below is derived from the Greek word *apoleia* meaning loss, destruction:

> *(27) Whatever happens, conduct yourselves in a manner worthy of the Gospel of Christ. Then, whether I come and see you or only hear about you in my absence, I will know that you stand firm in one spirit, contending as one man for the faith of the gospel (28) without being frightened in any way by those who oppose you. This is a sign to them that they will be destroyed, but that you will be saved--and that by God. (Philippians 1:27-28 NIV.)*

Again, Paul speaks of mankind's destruction. The root word for destruction is *alethros* meaning destruction, and the root word for perdition is *apoleia*:

> *But they that will be rich fall into temptation, into a snare, into many foolish and hurtful lusts, which plunge men into destruction and perdition. (1 Timothy 6:9 KJV.)*

Also describing eternal death of mankind in the following verse, the root word for perdition is *apoleia*. The connotation being those who are lost do not keep their souls:

> *But we are not of them who draw back unto perdition, but of them that believe to the saving of the soul. (Hebrews 10:39 KJV.)*

The root word for destruction in the following is also *apoleia*:

> *(13) Enter ye in at the straight gate; for wide is the gate, and broad is the way, that leadeth to destruction, and many there be which go in thereat, and the way is easy that leads to destruction, and those who enter by it are many. For the gate is narrow and the way is hard that leads to life, and those who find it are few. (14) Because strait is the gate, and narrow is the way, which leadeth unto life, and few there be that find it. (Matthew 7:13-14 KJV.)*

But eternal death is described best in the following verse. The root word for destruction is *apoleia*:

> *By the same word the present heavens and earth are reserved for fire, being kept for the day of judgment and destruction of ungodly men. (2 Peter 3:7. NIV.)*

The root word for kill below is the Greek word *apokteino*, meaning to kill entirely. And the root word for destroy is the Greek word *apollu*, meaning to lose off or away, destroy:

> *And fear not them which kill the body but are not able to kill the soul; but rather fear him which is able to destroy both soul and body in hell. (Matthew 10:28 KJV.)*

THE SECOND DEATH AND HELL

The King James Bible uses the word *lost* derived from the root word *apollu*, meaning to lose away, waste, destroy, instead of eternal death in the verse below:

> *If the Good News we preach is hidden to anyone, it is hidden from the one who is on the road to eternal death. (2 Corinthians 4:3.)*

And finally, the Scripture we all know best states that only through Christ shall we live; all others perish. The root word for perish is the Greek word *apollumi*, meaning to loose, loose away, destroy:

> *For God loved the world so much that he gave his only begotten Son so that anyone who believes in him shall not perish but have eternal life. (John 3:16.)*

What then have we learned about The Second Death and hell? Simply this: That clearly *Sheol* and *Hades* hell are temporary (Revelation 20:14-15) and are not the same as *Gehenna* hell; that all mankind, the righteous as well as the unrighteous, go bodily into *Sheol* and *Hades* hell (the grave) at the time of physical death, to remain there until resurrection and the judgments. After the judgments, the resurrected counted righteous go unto eternal life, and unredeemed mankind as well as fallen angels are thrown into the Lake of Fire, *Gehenna* hell. Therefore, *Gehenna* hell is the Lake of Fire, the everlasting Second Death from which there is no resurrection, ever.

Do you want to live? Man controls his own destiny. He has two choices! Man chooses to be thrown into the Lake of Fire in the eternal Second Death, or he chooses eternal life with God through Christ to live in incomprehensible glory throughout all eternity!

CHAPTER 14
ETERNITY

When eternity begins, the 1000-year reign of Christ has ended; all humanity has been judged; the Second Death has taken place. There will be no more death, pain, grief, disease, or heartache. Now it is time for all of God's people to receive untold blessings forever. The prophecy is that there will be a new earth. Listen to this!

(1) Then I saw a new earth (with no oceans) and a new sky, for the present earth and sky had disappeared. (2) And I, John, saw the Holy City, the new Jerusalem, coming down from God out of heaven. It was a glorious sight, beautiful as a bride at her wedding.

(3) I heard a loud shout from the throne saying, "Look, the home of God is now among men, and he will live with them, and they will be his people; yes, God himself will be among them. (4) He will wipe away all tears from their eyes, and there shall be no more death, nor sorrow, nor crying, nor pain. All of that has gone forever."

(5) And the one sitting on the throne said, "See, I am making all things new!" And then he said to me, "Write this down, for what I tell you is trustworthy and true: (6) It is finished! I am the A and the Z --the Beginning and the End. I will give to the thirsty the springs of the Water of Life--as a gift. (7) Everyone who conquers will inherit all these blessings, and I will be his God and he will be my son." (Revelation 21:1-7.)

Then John gives a glorious description of the New Jerusalem. It gives a glimpse of incomprehensible beauty:

(9) Then one of the seven angels who had emptied the flasks containing the seven last plagues came and said to me, "Come with me and I will show you the bride, the Lamb's

wife." (10) In a vision he took me to a towering mountain peak and from there I watched that wondrous city, the holy Jerusalem, descending out of the skies from God. (11) It was filled with the glory of God, and flashed and glowed like a precious gem, crystal clear like jasper.

(12) Its walls were broad and high, with twelve gates guarded by twelve angels. And the names of the twelve tribes of Israel were written on the gates. (13) There were three gates on each side--north, south, east, and west. (14) The walls had twelve foundation stones, and on them were written the names of the twelve apostles of the Lamb. (Revelation 21:9-14.)

Next John gives the size of the wondrous new city Jerusalem. Whether this is meant to be literal or symbolic, it depicts an enormous amount of room. Can you imagine a city 1500 miles square, the size of two or three of our states, with twelve layers or stories reaching 1500 miles high. That would be one and one-fourth miles between stories. This description of the New Jerusalem is one of incomprehensible spaciousness and beauty. What a magnificent sight that will be:

(15) The angel held in his hand a golden measuring stick to measure the city and its gates and walls. (16) When he measured it, he found it was a square as wide as it was long; in fact, it was in the form of a cube, for its height was exactly the same as its other dimensions--1500 miles each way. (17) Then he measured the thickness of the walls and found them to be 216 feet across (the angel called out these measurements to me, using standard units).

(18,19,20) The city itself was pure transparent gold like glass! The wall was made of jasper, and was built on twelve layers of foundations stones inlaid with gems: The first layer with jasper; the second with sapphire; the third with chalcedony; the fourth with emerald; the fifth with sardonyx; the sixth layer with sardus; the seventh with chrysolite; the eighth

with beryl; the ninth with topaz; the tenth with chrysoprase; the eleventh with jacinth; the twelfth with amethyst. (22) The twelve gates were made of pearls--each gate from a single pearl! And the main street was pure transparent gold, like glass. (Revelation 21:15-22.)

There will be no sun or moon or night, nor any need for sleep. So great is the incomprehensible glory of God and Christ that the light from the new holy city will light the whole world. And the rulers of the nations of the new earth bring their honor and glory to the holy city Jerusalem:

(22) No temple could be seen in the city, for the Lord God Almighty and the Lamb are worshiped in it everywhere. (23) And the city has no need of sun or moon to light it, for the glory of God and of the Lamb illuminate it. (24) Its light will light the nations of the earth, and the rulers of the world will come and bring their glory to it. (25) Its gates never close; they stay open all day long--and there is no night! (26) And the glory and honor of all the nations shall be bought into it. (27) Nothing evil will be permitted in it--no one immoral or dishonest--but only those whose names are written in the Lamb's Book of Life. (Revelation 21:22-27.)

Notice it specifies those in the **Lamb's Book of Life** will enjoy the privilege of inhabiting this new Jerusalem. How wonderful for Christians whose names are written in the Lamb's Book of Life.

Chapter 22 of the Book of Revelation describes more of the glories of eternity with God. It should be understood that the Scriptures in this study are only a few out of the Bible, and every person should study the whole Bible and the Book of Revelation in an honest and sincere effort to learn the truth of its meaning.

Rejoice for all Israel, and for all of God's people, for after testing through the trials and tribulations of this life, after judgment and punishment, this joyous eternity with God is their final and ultimate destiny. **Hallelujah!**

INDEX

CHAPTER 1. HOW DO WE KNOW CHRIST IS LORD
Number of years prophesied to Christ's first coming...Who is Daniel... Date of Christ's birth...new religion called The Way and Christians called the Sect of the Nazarenes...Believers first called Christians at Antioch...Proof of angels existence...Demons announced they knew Jesus...Crucifixion defined...Plan made for mankind's salvation before world was created...Suffering of early martyrs...How to gain eternal life...Value of the Kingdom of God...Assurance that salvation, once gained, cannot be lost...What is a true Christian.

CHAPTER 2. LUCIFER THE MAGNIFICENT, FALLEN.
Who is lucifer...The stones of fire...The Book of Enoch defined... Lucifer in Eden...Earth's creation reconciled to scientific data... Lucifer's fall...Christ is creator of angels...Description of angels... Number of angels...Fate of angels...Man's magic wand concept of creations...Measurements and foundation were laid for earth... Josephus' version of the creations...Reason for mankind's testing... Satan's accountability to God...The testing of Job...Destiny of Christ...Destiny of Satan...Plan of salvation hidden from angels... Fate of Lucifer.

CHAPTER 3. WHAT IS SIN?
The word sin means...The tragic consequences of sin...Remedy for sin.

CHAPTER 4. THE TRAGEDY OF ISRAEL.
Israel, God's chosen people...David chosen a king...Solomon inherited kingdom...Warning to Solomon...Kingdom of Israel divided...Promises to Jeroboam...Judgment of Jeroboam...Judgment of Israel...Destruction of Northern kingdom...Destruction of Southern kingdom...All Israel ceased to be a nation...The agony suffered during the siege on Jerusalem...Total destruction of Jerusalem...Israel's punishment...Definition of the Apocrypha...God looked at his spoilt world...Are Jews of today lost...God's fairness to the Jews...Israel's hope and final destiny...What is Israel's land...Muslims' Dome of the Rock...A nation reborn-Israel...Hosea's prophecy of length of time

until Israel's total restoration...Interviewing of the dispossessed, their sad plight...Israel retrieving their land...Weep for the Jew...Final punishment of Israel.

CHAPTER 5. WHO ARE THE ANTI-CHRIST AND FALSE PROPHET.
Who is the Anti-Christ...Who is the False Prophet...Daniel's prophecy of fallen world powers--Babylon, Medo-Persia, Greece, and Rome... The ten horns of Rome...The rise of the Anti-Christ and the False prophet...Who is the Notorious Prostitute...How to distinguish between the Anti-Christ and the real Jesus Christ.

CHAPTER 6. THE GREAT TRIBULATION.
Message to the churches...John's vision of the future...The seven-year treaty with Israel...Outline of the tribulation...Preparing to endure...When will the Rapture occur...Signal of Christ's second coming...How long will the holocausts last...The Seals...First Seal, peace achieved, populace deluded...Second Seal, peace treaty broken, war and killing, God's people defeated...Third Seal, world famine...Fourth Seal, one/fourth of world populace killed...Fifth Seal, slaughter of the Christians, how many...Mark of the Anti-Christ inflicted on world populace...Sixth Seal, sun becomes dark, moon red, stars appear to fall, marking of the 144,000...Seventh Seal, total silence, mighty angels line up to blow trumpets...The trumpets...First trumpet, one/third of earth set on fire...Second trumpet, one/third of all sea life killed...Third trumpet, one/third of all water poisoned, many people died...Fourth trumpet, one/third of sun, moon and stars obliterated, the three woes announced...Fifth trumpet, First woe, agony inflicted upon the ungodly...Sixth trumpet, Second woe, one/third of remaining mankind slaughtered, the two powerful witnesses killed and resurrected, terrible earthquake...Seventh trumpet, Third woe, the Rapture, what the resurrected body is like, end of the seven-year period...God's wrath...The Vials...First flask, horrible malignant sores...Second flask, all ocean life dies...Third flask, rivers become blood...Fourth flask, sun scorches mankind...Fifth flask, world plunged into darkness...Sixth flask, armies gathered for great Battle

INDEX

of Armageddon...Seventh flask, terrible earthquake, 100 pound hail, islands sink, mountains flatten out. Christ states, "It is finished."

CHAPTER 7. BETWEEN DEATH AND RESURRECTION
Where does the spirit go at the time of death...Paul looks forward to his heavenly body...Paul and disciples believed Christ would return during their lifetime...Righteous as well as the ungodly will be resurrected...Concept of soul returning to God at time of death...Josephus' Discourse to the Greeks Concerning Hades...Enoch describes Sheol (hell)...Ezra's version of Sheol (hell)...Concept of soul sleep...Lazarus raised from the dead...King David's request concerning his soul...Job's request concerning his soul.

CHAPTER 8. THE RESURRECTIONS.
Phases of the first resurrection...Resurrection of the two powerful witnesses...Resurrection of the 144,000...Resurrection of the Christians, the church...Glories of the resurrected body.

CHAPTER 9. THE JUDGMENT SEAT OF CHRIST.
Christians' judgment...Accountability of Christians...Christians beaten with stripes...Laying up treasures...Christians' rewards...Purifying of motives...Wedding banquet of Christ.

CHAPTER 10. THE SECOND COMING OF CHRIST.
Christ's second coming...Raptured Christians coming with Christ...Anti-Christ and False Prophet thrown alive into Lake of Fire...Armageddon.

CHAPTER 11. THE MILLENNIUM.
Judgment of the living...Who enters into the Millennium...Mourning of Israel...Death of King Josiah...There will be some death...Only sinners will die...No more wars...Crime not tolerated...Criminals executed...Christ rules with Rod of Iron...Christians also rule with Rod of Iron...Christ rules supreme...Finally peace and perfect justice...Inequities of life removed... Satan thrown into the Lake of Fire.

CHAPTER 12. THE GREAT WHITE THRONE JUDGMENT
Last resurrection...Great White Throne Judgment...God Almighty himself judges the dead...Books opened...Earth and heavens destroyed, burned up...Death and the grave (Sheol, Hades) destroyed.

CHAPTER 13. THE SECOND DEATH AND HELL
What is the Second Death? What is hell...How the word hell is used...The rich man and Lazarus...Concept of eternal torment... Concept of eternal death...No redemption for fallen angels...Angels await judgment in darkness...Satan's destruction...Anti-Christ's destruction...Destruction of ungodly mankind...What have we learned about hell...Do you want to live?

CHAPTER 14. ETERNITY
The new earth with no oceans...The New Jerusalem...Size of the New Jerusalem...Reason for rejoicing... Destiny of the Jews and all of God's people.

ENDNOTES

1. Zondervan Pictorial Bible Dictionary, Zondervan Publishing House, 5300 Patterson Avenue SE, Grand Rapids, Michigan 49530. 1967. Hardcover. Under Daniel. Pages 196-197.
2. Zondervan Pictorial Bible Dictionary, Zondervan Publishing House, 5300 Patterson Avenue SE, Grand Rapids, Michigan 49530. 1967. Hardcover. Under Jeremiah. Page 410.
3. Zondervan Pictorial Bible Dictionary, Zondervan Publishing House, 5300 Patterson Avenue SE, Grand Rapids, Michigan 49530. 1967. Hardcover. Under Zechariah. Page 909.
4. Foxe Book of Martyrs, Whitaker House, 30 Hunt Valley Circle, New Kensington, Pennsylvania 15068. Paperback. Pages 18, 26, 28.
5. Zondervan Pictorial Bible Dictionary, Zondervan Publishing House, 5300 Patterson Avenue SE, Grand Rapids, Michigan 49530. 1967. Hardcover. Under Nero. Page 581.
6. Zondervan Pictorial Bible Dictionary, Zondervan Publishing House, 5300 Patterson Avenue SE, Grand Rapids, Michigan 49530. 1967. Hardcover. Under Cross. Page 189.
7. The Book of Enoch, Wip & Stock Publishers, 199 W. 8th Avenue, Suite 3, Eugene, Oregon 97402.
8. Zondervan Pictorial Bible Dictionary, Zondervan Publishing House, 5300 Patterson Avenue SE, Grand Rapids, Michigan 49530. 1967. Hardcover. Under Books of Enoch. Page 252.
9. The Expanded Panorama Bible Study Course, Fleming H. Revell, a division of Baker Book House Company, P.O. Box 6287, Grand Rapids, Michigan 49516-6287. 1994. Paperback. Page 23.
10. The World Book Encyclopedia, World Book Publishing, 233 N. Michigan, Suite 2000, Chicago, Illinois 60601. 1996. Volume 6, Page 24, 26; Volume 4, Page 636; Volume 5, Page 207.
11. The Expanded Panorama Bible Study Course, Fleming H. Revell, a division of Baker Book House Company, P.O. Box 6287, Grand Rapids, Michigan 49516-6287. 1994. Paperback. Page 19.
12. The Book of Enoch, Wip & Stock Publishers, 199 W. 8th Avenue, Suite 3, Eugene, Oregon 97401. Paperback. Page 46.
13. The Book of Enoch, Wip & Stock Publishers, 199 W. 8th Avenue, Suite 3, Eugene, Oregon 97401. Paperback. Page 44.
14. The Works of Josephus, Antiquities of the Jews, Translated by William Whiston, A.M., Hendrickson Publishers, Inc., P.O. Box 3473, Peabody, Massachusetts 01961-3473. 1989. Hardcover. Page 30.
15. Zondervan Pictorial Bible Dictionary, Zondervan Publishing House, 5300 Patterson Avenue SE, Grand Rapids, Michigan 49530. 1967. Hardcover. Under sin. Page 796.

16. Zondervan Pictorial Bible Dictionary, Zondervan Publishing House, 5300 Patterson Avenue SE, Grand Rapids, Michigan 49530. 1967. Hardcover. Under David. Pages 201, 203.
17. The Works of Josephus, Antiquities of the Jews, Translated by William Whiston, A.M., Hendrickson Publishers, Inc., P.O. Box 3473, Peabody, Massachusetts 01961-3473. 1989. Hardcover. Book 18. Chapter I, Pages 477-478. Book 5. Chapter 4, Pages 703-705.
18. Zondervan Pictorial Bible Dictionary, Zondervan Publishing House, 5300 Patterson Avenue SE, Grand Rapids, Michigan 49530. 1967. Hardcover. Under Titus. Page 587.
19. The Works of Josephus, Wars of the Jews, Translated by William Whiston, A.M., Hendrickson Publishers, Inc., P.O. Box 3473, Peabody, Massachusetts 01961-3473. 1989. Hardcover. Book 5. Chapter 10, Page 719; Chapter 11, Page 721; Chapter 12, Pages 723-724; Chapter 13, Page 725.
20. The Works of Josephus, Wars of the Jews, Translated by William Whiston, A.M., Hendrickson Publishers, Inc., P.O. Box 3473, Peabody, Massachusetts 01961-3473. 1989. Hardcover. Book 6. Chapters 1 through 8, Pages 727-748; Chapter 9, Pages 748-749.
21. Zondervan Pictorial Bible Dictionary, Zondervan Publishing House, 5300 Patterson Avenue SE, Grand Rapids, Michigan 49530. 1967. Hardcover. Under Jerusalem. Page 423.
22. Random House Webster's College Dictionary, Random House, Inc., 1745 Broadway, New York, New York 10019. 1996. Hardcover. Page 65.
23. The New English Bible, The Apocrypha, 1970. Cambridge University Press, 40 W. 20th Street, New York, New York 10011-4211. 1970. Hardcover.
24. Zondervan Pictorial Bible Dictionary, Zondervan Publishing House, 5300 Patterson Avenue SE, Grand Rapids, Michigan 49530. 1967. Hardcover. Under Hittites. Page 356. Under Philistines. Page 651.
25. Zondervan Pictorial Bible Dictionary, Zondervan Publishing House, 5300 Patterson Avenue SE, Grand Rapids, Michigan 49530. 1967. Hardcover. Under Jerusalem. Pages 423-424.
26. Zondervan Pictorial Bible Dictionary, Zondervan Publishing House, 5300 Patterson Avenue SE, Grand Rapids, Michigan 49530. 1967. Hardcover. Under Alexander the Great. Pages 28-29.
27. There is a New World Coming, Harvest House Publishers, 990 Owen Loop North, Eugene, Oregon 97402. Copyright returned to Hal Lindsey Website Ministries, P.O. Box 1131, Murrieta, California 92564. Paperback. Chapter 13, Page 192.
28. The Works of Josephus, Discourse to the Greeks Concerning Hades, Translated by William Whiston, A.M., Hendrickson Publishers, Inc., P.O. Box 3473, Peabody, Massachusetts 01961-3473. 1989. Hardback. Pages 813-814.
29. The Book of Enoch, Wip & Stock Publishers, 199 W. 8th Ave, Suite 3, Eugene, Oregon, 97401. 1987. Paper back. Chapter XXII, Page 47.

ENDNOTES

30. The New English Bible, The Apocrypha, Cambridge University Press, 40 W. 20th Street, New York, New York 10011-4211. 1970. Hardcover.
31. Young's Analytical Concordance to the Bible, Thomas Nelson Publishers, P.O. Box 141000, Nashville, Tennessee 37214. 1980. Hardcover. Under grave. Page 432. Under hell. Page 474. Under pit. Page 753. Under torment. Page 995.
32. Divine Plan, What Say the Scriptures Concerning Hell, P.O. Box 4085, Fort Worth, Texas 76106. Page 11.
33. The Works of Josephus, Discourse to the Greeks Concerning Hades, Translated by William Whiston, A.M., Hendrickson Publishers. Inc., P.O. Box 3473, Peabody, Massachusetts 01961-3473. Hardcover. Pages 813-814.

ABOUT THE AUTHOR

Charlene Roberson Chandler is a native Texan and teacher of Bible study classes in churches for over 35 years. Employed by the Department of Army at Fort Wolters, Texas from 1962 to 1974. Upon base closure, attended and graduated from Chapman Court Reporting College in Fort Worth, Texas. Relocated to Forrest City, Arkansas in 1979 for employment in the First Judicial Circuit of Eastern Arkansas as an official court reporter for the Honorable Henry Wilkinson, retiring in 1995. Married to James Chandler. Children consist of three wonderful step-children and one son Mark who resides in Seattle with his wife and two daughters. Hobbies consist of oil painting, writing, reading, sewing, and flower gardening.